T0312031

A Career is a Promise: Finding Purpose, Success, and Fulfillment levels the playing field by providing a road map to the realization of a career. From setting realistic goals and mitigating rejection to navigating the bumpy road to cultural competence, this book guides you through an interactive process of self-discovery and goal-generating activities as you prepare to enter the job market. It is a must-read for young multidisciplinary professionals starting or changing careers.

> **Audrey G. Bennett,** *University Diversity and Social Transformation Professor, Penny W. Stamps School of Art & Design, University of Michigan*

In a time when technology and innovation rapidly alter the workplace landscape, Prof. Landa offers a guide for finding your purpose in the promise you make to your career. The blend of reflection exercises and assessments with her personal story and interviews will inspire you to define your career journey in a unique way. As a former university career services director, organization consultant, and management professor, I highly recommend this book to you regardless of your career phase: new job entrant, career pivoter or an emerging retiree. It will serve you well throughout the arc of your career.

> **Mary Cianni, PhD,** *Adjunct Faculty, MS in Executive Coaching and Organizational Consulting, New York University*

Finding one's career path, let alone a career passion involves reflection, research, and a plan. This positive guide comes with road maps, self-assessments, and clear directives on attaining a fulfilling career by design, not a career by happenstance.

> **Nicole Van Den Heuvel,** *Executive Director, Center for Career Development, Rice University, Houston, Texas*

From tips on identifying your purpose, cultural intelligence to cultivating mentors and sponsors, this book is packed with invaluable insights that will help readers achieve their career goals. Highly recommended!

> **Bernice Chao,** *Co-author of the award-winning book The Visibility Mindset*

Through diverse interviews and personal experience, Landa diligently makes us pause to analyze, and take charge of our lives with sensitivity and reflection. How we can better cultivate cultural and emotional intelligence, become upstanders advocating for multicultural perspectives, lead with empathy, and find contentment.

Archana Shekara, *Professor of Graphic Design, Creative Director of Design Streak Studio, Co-director of Ethnic Studies at Illinois State University, and Founding Member of South Asian Design Educators Alliance (SADEA)*

Robin Landa's book is an outstanding set of road maps, prompts, and inner-directed questions to guide you on how you can choose to spend a significant proportion of your adult years. Your career!! Your career or job is a substantial aspect of self-definition. While parents, celebrities, and professionals are often our role models, and often major shapers of our career choices, Landa makes clear that many factors, some conscious, some unconscious, and some determination, determine our choice of job or career. And looking at our choices or lack thereof can enhance the work stage of life. With wisdom from successful others, and from her own work with university students and others, she delightfully introduces us to a world of insights, and hope for meaningful career choices. Any adult young or old contemplating career choices can profit from this book. As a psychologist in practice for 50 years, this book helped me to retake the driver's seat in my career and contemplation of what I can still do to enhance it!

Barbara L. Blum, PhD, *psychologist*

Landa's new book contains essential advice for job seekers. It helps those searching for a career identify their core values, nonnegotiables and gets at the heart of why they are applying to certain positions. The worksheets, checklists, and other interactive elements help readers to identify their needs and wants so they can articulate those desires during an interview. In addition to all the helpful guidance and activities, there are interviews with professionals sharing their career experience and advice throughout, which puts a real-world emphasis on the process and lets the reader know they are not alone in the job search. After doing the activities in this book, readers will understand what they truly want in a career and how to be successful in the process of finding the right employment match.

Dr. Tricia M. Farwell, *Associate Professor, School of Journalism, Middle Tennessee State University*

Landa just wrote the book we've all been waiting for; so critical, it should be in the hands of everyone. Simply pragmatic, this intentional guide brings diverse voices and sage wisdom to anyone looking to own the adventure of a purpose-filled life far beyond work.

Herb Vincent Peterson, *Associate Professor of Design, South Carolina School of the Arts, Anderson University*

Robin has been a fantastic guest on my podcast. She has written a book detailing the journey towards career success and fulfillment. The journey to a successful career is no longer the straight 9-5, commute, Ivy League, corporate ladder pathway anymore. It takes careful introspection, definition of values, and what you will and will not accept in the workplace. There are some interviews with fantastic guests in there. Definitely worth checking out, for anyone interested in making more of an impact in today's world.

Christopher H. Loo, MD-PhD, *Founder and CEO of Financial Freedom for Physicians Podcast*

A Career is a Promise goes beyond the ordinary career guides. Its universal appeal is rooted in its ability to transcend disciplines and industries, making it an ideal gift for a fresh-faced graduate unsure of their next steps or an experienced professional seeking a fulfilling second career.

NiRey Reynolds, *Global Director of Creative Excellence, Momentum Worldwide*

As a marketer and career mentor for the past 20 years, *A Career is a Promise* brings a fresh perspective to the current professional branding and planning space. Bringing creativity, vision and a road map for success for students and professionals alike.

Donna Wertalik, M.S. *Marketing, Director of Marketing Strategy & Analytics, Pamplin College of Business, Professor of Practice, Marketing Department, Virginia Tech*

A Career is a Promise

No matter your field of interest, *A Career is a Promise* offers a proven framework for finding purpose, success, and fulfillment. Robin Landa, one of the world's leading experts on creativity and idea generation, reveals practical strategies that will help you identify a career worthy of your intelligence, aptitudes, and time.

Much more than a how-to guide, the road maps, prompts, inner-directed questions, and self-assessment tools will help you discover what most excites you professionally, set worthwhile career goals, find purpose in your career, achieve success, lead with compassion, find fulfillment, secure mentors and sponsors, and enhance your creative thinking to best compete in a global marketplace.

Most of us don't spend adequate time thinking about what ignites our souls and makes our careers roar—well enough to forge a fruitful and satisfying career path. When you spend more than one-third of your life working, your career should hold promise. A career is a promise you make to yourself.

Robin Landa is a distinguished professor at Kean University and a globally recognized creativity and ideation expert. She is a best-selling author of books on idea generation, creativity, branding, advertising, and design. She has won numerous awards, and The Carnegie Foundation counts her among the "Great Teachers of Our Time." She is the author of twenty-five books, including *Graphic Design Solutions*, 6th ed., *Strategic Creativity*, and *The New Art of Ideas. Harvard Business Review, Inc. Magazine,* and

Fast Company, among others, have published her articles. Through her teaching, writing, mentoring, and presentations, Landa has had a profound impact on thousands of careers, inspiring and educating countless creative professionals, CCOs, and CMOs, helping to shape thousands of successful careers.

A Career is a Promise

Finding Purpose, Success, and Fulfillment

Robin Landa

Routledge
Taylor & Francis Group
NEW YORK AND LONDON

Front and back Cover Design: Ana Carolina Mitchell

Chapter opener design: Ana Carolina Mitchell

First published 2024
by Routledge
605 Third Avenue, New York, NY 10158

and by Routledge
4 Park Square, Milton Park, Abingdon, Oxon, OX14 4RN

Routledge is an imprint of the Taylor & Francis Group, an Informa business

© 2024 Robin Landa

The right of Robin Landa to be identified as author of this work has been asserted in accordance with sections 77 and 78 of the Copyright, Designs and Patents Act 1988.

Library of Congress Cataloging-in-Publication Data
Names: Landa, Robin, author.
Title: A career is a promise: finding purpose, success, and fulfillment / Robin Landa.
Description: New York, NY: Routledge, 2024. | Includes bibliographical references and index. |
Identifiers: LCCN 2023025225 (print) | LCCN 2023025226 (ebook) | ISBN 9781032496948 (hardback) | ISBN 9781032496931 (paperback) | ISBN 9781003395034 (ebook)
Subjects: LCSH: Vocational guidance. | Creative thinking. | Success in business.
Classification: LCC HF5381 .L2886 2024 (print) | LCC HF5381 (ebook) | DDC 650.1--dc23/eng/20230821
LC record available at https://lccn.loc.gov/2023025225
LC ebook record available at https://lccn.loc.gov/2023025226

ISBN: 978-1-032-49694-8 (hbk)
ISBN: 978-1-032-49693-1 (pbk)
ISBN: 978-1-003-39503-4 (ebk)

DOI: 10.4324/9781003395034

Typeset in Sabon
by SPi Technologies India Pvt Ltd (Straive)

A Career is a Promise is dedicated to you, dear Reader. May you find purpose, success, and fulfillment in your career.

Contents

About the Author

Robin Landa is a distinguished professor at Kean University and a globally recognized creativity, design, advertising, and ideation expert. She is a best-selling author of books on idea generation, creativity, branding, advertising, and design. She has won numerous awards, and The Carnegie Foundation counts her among the "Great Teachers of Our Time." She is the author of twenty-five books including *Graphic Design Solutions*, 6th ed., *Strategic Creativity: A Business Field Guide to Advertising, Branding, and Design*, *Advertising by Design: Generating and Designing Ideas Across Media*, 4th ed., and *The New Art of Ideas: Unlock Your Creative Potential*. She is currently co-authoring a book for Columbia University Press titled, *Shareworthy: Advertising that Creates Powerful Connections through Storytelling*. Robin is a former chair of Design Incubation and serves as a creative consultant to the C-suites of international corporations. Through her teaching, writing, mentoring, and speaking, Landa has had a profound impact on the fields of graphic design, branding, and advertising, inspiring and educating countless creative professionals, CCOs, and CMOs, and helping to shape thousands of successful careers. You can visit her website at: Robinlanda.com.

Foreword

By **Dr. Heidi K. Gardner**, Distinguished Fellow at Harvard Law School and Co-founder of Gardner & Co.

With people spending up to one-third of their life working, this time had better be meaningful. But recent developments like the COVID-19 pandemic, hybrid working, and a global mental health crisis have made it even harder to connect with others and embody that sense of purpose. Robin Landa's *A Career is a Promise: Finding Purpose, Success, and Fulfillment* arrives at the perfect moment, offering proven, easy-to-digest tips and tools for finding fulfillment in our careers—and our lives in general.

I know firsthand the value of discovering a fruitful and fulfilling career path. As a distinguished fellow at Harvard Law School, best-selling author, and advisor for companies across the globe, I've built a career around my top passion: collaboration. As Landa explores in her book, amazing things happen when people with different knowledge bases, backgrounds, and personality traits come together to tackle a problem (what my team and I call smarter collaboration). This exciting phenomenon has guided my vocational choices, even if my path hasn't been orthodox. I went from studying Japanese at the University of Pennsylvania, to embarking on the management track at Procter & Gamble, to consulting at McKinsey & Company in London and South Africa—by way of a Fulbright fellowship in Germany and a master's at the London School of Economics. I ultimately ended up with a PhD from London Business School and an academic career at Harvard;

through all these experiences, understanding and following my "North Star" led me to the success and joy I experience today.

In *A Career is a Promise*, Landa offers a series of questions to help the reader determine their guiding lights—including values, interests, and goals. By reflecting on what excites you the most professionally, aligning with your talents, core principles, and desired work environment, you can run with that knowledge and determine your next steps—big and small. Landa explores how this insight doesn't just help individuals: it also enhances teams, allowing everyone to play to their strengths (a core tenant of effective collaboration).

The book contains rich and inspiring examples of successful individuals leveraging their strengths and sense of purpose. For example, Dr. Joan Fallon, founder and CEO of Curemark, has focused her career on bettering the health of children—and most recently treating autism. And Ilana Kloss, CEO of Billie Jean King Enterprises, has pursued her love for tennis—first as a professional tennis player and now on creating opportunities for underrepresented communities in sports. A complementary message is that while specialization is important, having different experiences and interests (for example, hobbies, board roles, and even side hustles) better equips people to lead and solve problems.

Landa offers research-based advice for leaders *and* those they manage. She drives home the point that people shouldn't wait for top-down initiatives to boost diversity and inclusion, and in turn feelings of engagement and belonging. Instead, they can take it upon themselves—no matter their level—to deliberately bring a range of colleagues into the conversation. By demonstrating inclusivity time and time again, they make it a bigger part of their organization's culture. This doesn't just benefit others; it also helps them connect, learn, and perform better.

Another ticket to satisfaction and success at work is finding the right mentors and sponsors. Landa offers fresh ideas for procuring and maintaining these relationships, some of which are grounded in the principles of smarter collaboration (for example, clearly communicating your goals, being open to working with people outside your organization, demonstrating trustworthiness, creating meeting agendas). Effective collaboration concepts also show up in the chapter about being a good leader. These include traits like self-awareness, self-regulation, and openness to others' opinions.

Whether you're just starting off your career, or with many years of experience under your belt, *A Career is a Promise* is full of valuable lessons and exercises. Learn how to get to know yourself better, and from there the opportunity for more collaborative, meaningful, and impactful work only grows.

Acknowledgments

I am grateful to so many people for contributing to this book.

Many of the world's most accomplished leaders in their fields—Anita Schjøll Abildgaard, Dr. Arti Agrawal, Dr. Juliet Bourke, Dr. Joan Fallon, Dr. Heather Frederick, Gabriel Fuentes, Sophie Gold, Lee-Sean Huang, Harsh Kapadia, Ilana Kloss, Zoia Kozakov, Eoin McLaughlin, PJ Pereira, Mark S. Robinson, Dr. Chris E. Stout, Sonya Renee Taylor, and Dr. Carl M. Truesdale—were willing to take time away from their vast professional responsibilities to share their expertise to contribute to this book. I am not just grateful to each of them for their generous support, but humbled, encouraged, and awed by all that they do.

As if this weren't enough, this book is graced with a Foreword written by Dr. Heidi Gardner, Distinguished Fellow at Harvard Law School and Co-founder of Gardner & Co. Her expertise and insights are invaluable. I am honored to have Dr. Gardner's endorsement. She is a role model for us all.

At Routledge, I am eternally grateful to Meredith Norwich for her professionalism, support, kindness, and unwavering commitment to excellence. To Bethany Nelson and Edward Taylor, thank you very much for your great support. Thank you to Samar Haddad, copyeditor, and to Aishwariya Madhana Shankar, project manager at Straive.

For their kindness and support, I extend my thanks to Audrey G. Bennett, Dr. Jill Bellinson, Dr. Barbara Blum, Kevin Brainard, Steven Brower, Bernice Chao, Mary Cianni, Denise Corazza, Andrew

Doran, Christine Dunne, Justin Epstein, Dr. Tricia Farwell, Emma Ford, Hayley Gruenspan, Nicole Van Den Heuvel, Jordie Inoa, Dr. Christopher H. Loo, Fernando Mattei, Tip Nunn, Herb Vincent Peterson, NiRey Reynolds, Archana Shekara, Patrycja Sliwowska, Emma Swanson, and Donna Wertalik.

At Kean University, I am grateful to Dr. Lamont Repollet, president; Dr. David Birdsell, provost and senior vice president of academic affairs; David Mohney, dean, Michael Graves College; Rose Gonnella, associate dean, Michael Graves College; Reenat Munshi and the office of Research and Sponsored Programs; Prof. Deborah Ceballos; and all of my Michael Graves College colleagues and students.

Great thanks to Ana Carolina Mitchell, who designed the fabulous cover and chapter openers—you have a brilliant career ahead of you.

I am deeply grateful to my husband Harry, whose dedication to his own career has been a constant source of inspiration for me; I admire him for his commitment to excellence, hard work, and the joy he finds in the practice of medicine. Harry is my hero.

To all and for all, I am grateful.

I've enjoyed a fruitful career and have guided thousands of university students who now enjoy satisfying careers in extremely competitive creative professions. May you find purpose, success, and fulfillment.

INTRODUCTION

DOI: 10.4324/9781003395034-1

Predicting Your Future

Look into your crystal ball and tell me…

"Where do you see yourself in five years?" That's a customary question prospective employers ask when they interview someone for a job, almost certainly at the start of one's career. Essentially, they are asking you to predict what you will want to be doing years from that exact moment, and using your answer to decide if you're getting the job.

What these employers really want to know is your intentions, whether you intend to stick around, where you see yourself in their organization in the longer term, or whether the job they're about to offer is merely a means of advancement to a bigger and better career. Giving them the benefit of the doubt, perhaps the interviewer is truly interested in knowing you better, for example your goals and your passions, or assessing whether they'd like to have coffee with you in the break room.

That common interview question is also commonly challenging to answer, unless you're the upstart who, in five years, sees yourself as a partner in a law firm, designing grand office buildings, or being a showrunner for a prestige television program. For most people at the start of their careers, it's difficult to know precisely what they want to be doing in five years, or for the rest of their professional lives for that matter. Why can't you simply hit the "don't know yet" button?

And, "don't know yet" is a very reasonable reply, as career aspirations follow various paths: straight, zig-zagging, circuitous, along with pivots. For many of us, career goals change, too, earlier or later on.

It's likely you have a strong desire to be successful or you wouldn't be reading this; however, all of us often cite aspirations very loosely, perhaps as achieving something great or becoming rich or famous. Of course, you aspire to do great things but exactly what, why, and how? (Though I envy the person who doesn't and just wants peace of mind and a paycheck.)

Or perhaps you do know the answer. For now. Trust me when I tell you that careers don't always follow a straight and obstacle-free path from the ideal to actuality.

Let's back up to that interview in the beginning. Why were you applying for that job or any job? Pick one:

- It's the opportunity of a lifetime
- It's the entry point to the career I desire
- My family or friend made me apply
- I need a job to pay the rent
- Pretty random
- None of the above

If you selected "My family or friend made me apply," "Pretty random," or "None of the above," you have a lot of company. The tools in this book will help you ascertain why.

Taking any job to pay the rent, of course, is what many of us must do. Fair. However, let's see if we can get you to realize which jobs would be more attuned to your aptitudes, thinking, and ambitions.

If you selected "It's the opportunity of a lifetime," or "It's the entry point to the career I desire," then you know how to kick-start your career; however, let's make sure you

- determine your values,
- manifest your purpose,
- set your goals well enough to grow,
- act as an upstanding citizen of your workplace,
- tap into the leader within,
- find a mentor and sponsor,
- feel fulfilled, and
- find success.

That's where the tools in this book come in. Most importantly, they will lead to more self-discovery, as most of us don't spend adequate time thinking about what ignites our souls and makes careers tick and roar—well enough to forge a fruitful and fulfilling career path.

The time you put into answering the questions in this book is equivalent to winning a lottery. Okay, well it's hard to beat winning a huge jackpot all at once but you'll definitely gain in the long run.

What This Book Offers You

You might be born to sing. Or born to code. You might know your life goal or purpose. Creating an actionable career road map, without a doubt, ensures fulfillment. Think of this book as your career coach providing thought-provoking tools and content to help you work out what you'd like to do and achieve, and how to thrive.

Much more than a how-to career guide, the content, roadmaps, prompts, inner-directed questions, and self-assessment tools will help you transform your thinking in order to:

- Map a North Star to guide your career
- Honor your potential and values
- Realize your purpose
- Set life, macro- and micro-goals for personal and professional growth
- Cultivate your cultural intelligence
- Advocate for diversity, equity, and inclusion
- Secure career-making relationships with mentors and sponsors
- Find success and fulfillment
- Become an effective leader
- Lead with compassion
- Unleash your creativity
- Get priceless career advice from interviews with esteemed professionals
- Discover your authenticity through numerous self-assessment exercises and enlightening tools—digging deep to find purpose, success, and fulfillment

Audiences and Uses

This book is a step-by-step road map to identifying and crystallizing a satisfying career. Although appropriate for almost anyone, it is geared toward five types of audiences:

- Individuals in a professional, technical, or creative role who want a promising and fulfilling career will find this book valuable in helping them identify their guiding North Star, values, purpose, and goals (big and small) based on their own aspirations or in helping them make progress in a career or an organization.
- Independent consultants, external or internal, will find this book valuable for their growth and success because, now more than ever, we are in a new era of artificial general intelligence that forces us to examine what a career looks like. This audience includes consultants, coaches, contractors, counselors, mentors, and advisors who need to demonstrate their ability to contribute to the growth and progress of a business, organization, or community, and to help people find authenticity, become leaders, and think creatively. This book provides the keys to unlocking clients' career potential.
- Experienced professionals will find this book helpful to finding purpose, success, and fulfillment. Some professionals, even those with a wealth of experience, may be stuck in a stagnant position where they are not flourishing, and that is not authentic to who they truly are. This book shows how to broaden your thinking to gain the recognition and success you deserve.
- Leaders, team leaders, managers, and project managers will find this book a valuable resource for guiding their employees and teams and enhancing team performance across the board. In most cases, a team's work reflects the team leader's performance. They can also use Chapter 5 on cultivating cultural intelligence and diversity, equity, and inclusion (DEI) to improve their workplace.

- Faculty in almost every field assist their students to find worthwhile career paths. The self-assessment tools are easy for college and university students to implement—I know this because I use them effectively in my classroom. I've taught thousands of university students who have gone on to rewarding careers. Alumni tell me that this process helps them secure the careers they desire, stay ahead of their peers on the job, and advance quickly.

Self-knowledge is powerful, comprising not only your beliefs concerning your actual self but also your expectations for your future—for who you might become. You do have "possible selves," what you perceive as potentially possible with regard to your future.[1] This book will help you, dear reader, get to know your actual self and your possible selves and realize the wonderful possibilities.

Welcome to *A Career is a Promise: Finding Purpose, Success, and Fulfillment*. Because everyone is worthy of a rewarding career!

Note

1 Markus H, Nurius P, "Possible Selves," *American Psychologist*, 41(9), 954–969. https://doi.org/10.1037/0003-066X.41.9.954

A CAREER BY DESIGN

DOI: 10.4324/9781003395034-2

Your Promise to Yourself

A career is a promise.

You have a reason to expect something from your career that goes beyond a paycheck—the expectation of success, growth, as well as being treated fairly. Of course, we expect our employer to be the one keeping their promise, but beyond your promise to fulfill your obligations to your employer, *what's your promise to yourself?*

Careers hold promise. In order to fulfill their promise and to realize your potential and all possibilities, make a promise to yourself through your personal code by scrutinizing your desires to determine what you truly want to do, setting relevant goals, and allowing your aspirations to guide you.

When you mindfully examine your values, purpose, and greatest assets and skills, define and prioritize your goals, determine what drives you, realize the kind of environment you want to work in, find what truly brings fulfillment into your life, and establish career-making relationships, *then success follows.*

Sure, some people tend to equate success with wealth, fame, or power. Staying true to yourself, making full use of your intelligence, training, talent, and skills, finding meaning in what you do, finding mentors and sponsors who will support and advocate for you, and realizing your full potential are other ways to define success.

A Career by Design

Part of my role as a university professor is advising graduates on career paths. My graduating seniors express common concerns and questions including: whether to work for a small, mid-sized, or large organization; whether they will be happy in a specific role; where to start their career journey; whether they need a mentor and sponsor; how to become an early leader; how to win the respect of their peers and supervisors; and what type of company culture would suit them. Here is the advice that has helped thousands (and I mean literally thousands) of my former students find fulfillment and success in very competitive careers.

Think of me as your career advisor—enabling you to better understand your purpose, strengths, skills, and desires so that you can align them with a career.

Design your career. Decide what you want. Not so easy, right? That's where identifying your *core purpose*—an enduring intention to achieve a life goal—and your career's North Star come in. Perhaps you see your core purpose very generally, for example, as helping others. Or you specifically know you were born to code, or a combo thereof. Either way, gaining clarity is illuminating and directional.

Your North Star serves as a motivational purpose guide, to keep you on a course that is aligned with your core principles and your life goal. Always remember, you are the hero of your own career.

Set your career goals. To fulfill your purpose or achieve a life goal, you need to plan phased career goals to get you where you want to be. (If you claim you're winging it, good for you. However, I'd bet you've tucked big and small goals in there without calling what you're doing a plan, for example, earning a university degree or learning a new skill. Just saying.) Basically, there are two types of career goals that you set for yourself: macro-goals and micro-goals (or concurrent goals). To attain what you desire and feel fulfilled in any role, you need to set and achieve both types of goals.

Recognizing which goals are important, the ones that feed your purpose and growth and move you along your career path, is key. There are many self-assessment tools in this book to help you plan the steps, rewards, and sacrifices necessary to achieve all of your career goals.

Cultivate your cultural intelligence. You bring a worldview to your career, and other people bring theirs. Cultivating your cultural intelligence will ensure smarter collaboration, collegiality, and learning. Becoming an upstander—someone who advocates for diversity, equity, and inclusion—and widening your lens to obtain diverse perspectives ensures equity, greater understanding, teamwork, and better ideas and solutions.

Ensure success. One way to secure success is through career-making relationships. Obtaining a mentor who provides career guidance and a sponsor who advocates for your advancement can help you achieve success. When a sponsor believes in your capabilities and advocates for you, you're more likely to be noticed and advance.

Unleash the leader within. Developing leadership attributes and skills early on can help you land more opportunities and have more influence.

Effective leaders are intelligent experts who are wise, fair, decent, compassionate, good listeners, and effective communicators, and who encourage dialogue. Whether you want to be in charge, be promoted, or have influence, adopting early leadership characteristics and cultivating your emotional intelligence are a fast track to success.

Find fulfillment in your career and life. Finding work that you believe is worth your investment and that addresses your interests, expertise, and talent is a worthwhile pursuit. Perhaps it's the alignment of all of those elements that lead to finding fulfillment in a career. It's definitely not the same for everyone, nor does it necessarily remain constant over the course of one's life. Self-discovery and self-evaluation provide sufficient insight to chart a meaningful career path and provide agency—putting you in charge of your career. Aside from your full-time job, fulfillment can be found in passion projects or side hustles where you can put your interests and skills to another use.

The purpose of this book is to make you better understand your purpose, aspirations, capabilities, goals, and everything you have to offer and want, so that you can align them and design an actionable career path tailored to finding purpose, success, and fulfillment.

Your Nonnegotiables

As a prelude to setting professional goals, it helps to identify what is important to you in life, in other words your values and standards. Let's call these your nonnegotiables. In other words, in order to live with yourself, what won't you compromise?

As journalist and author S. Mitra Kalita said in a speech to graduates at Columbia University,

> Someone, at some point, will ask you to do the wrong thing. It is in those moments you must figure out what you stand for. Who are you willing to speak up for? To fight for? What are you willing to quit over? It helps to find someone or something that centers you. In my case, it's my family—my kids are my moral anchors. They cuddle up with me in the bed in the morning and I never want to do anything that compromises the purity of that moment.[1]

American psychologist Abraham Maslow presented his theory of human motivation (in a paper in 1943 and later penned a book in 1954) proposing five core needs that form the basis for human motivation and therefore influence people's behavior. Maslow arranged the five needs into a pyramid, with physiological needs (air, water, food, sleep, etc.) at the bottom, followed by security needs (safety, stability), social needs (love, belonging), ego needs (self-esteem, recognition), and finally, at the pinnacle, self-actualization needs (development, creativity).

As psychologist Dr. Jill Bellinson pointed out to me, when you're concerned about basic physiological needs or issues, such as having enough food, having shelter, and feeling safe, then fulfilling your passion at work isn't a priority. Once physiological and security needs are fulfilled, people want to fulfill their social, ego, and self-actualization needs, for example, to belong, to have friends and family (related to survival and companionship), to have love interests (related to sex drive and companionship), to be invigorated (related to motivation and amusement), to experience things (related to curiosity), and more.

Once basic needs are met, we are free to be concerned with our foundational values and the standards of behavior we want to uphold as individuals—principles that matter to us. Your values help to define your goals. They also help to motivate you. Very often, these values become nonnegotiable no matter the job.

> Just stay true to your values and your principles. Simple as that.
> —Keith Wandell, president and CEO of Harley-Davidson, Inc.[2]

Personal Code

Portia, one of my graduating seniors, was overjoyed when a New York City advertising agency offered her a junior art director position—a career path exactly corresponding to what she had majored in at Kean University. She accepted the position. After a couple of weeks, Portia contacted me to say she had left that agency because she did not want to create compelling advertising for a cigarette brand; she took a parallel position at a different ad agency that did not have cigarette brands as clients. Although that happened many years ago, I never forgot Portia acting on her moral compass.

Portia lives by a personal code (or ethos) that embraces beneficence—an obligation to others to do no harm. Call it ethics, values, moral values, or a code of conduct; whatever you call it, articulated or lived, your personal code governs the choices you make. A career is a promise for fulfilling work, not a compromise of your code.

> I have standards I don't plan on lowering for anybody … including myself.
>
> —Zendaya, actor and singer

Your personal code guides your actions and sets your standards, too; it contributes to your guiding North Star (which we'll explore in Chapter 2). Your standards might have been shaped by your own sense of right and wrong and duty, by your family and community, your religion, or your belief system. Your career code of conduct will undoubtedly be influenced by all that has shaped you to your core. Certain aspects of your code likely will be immutable; however, some might need to be flexible in order to be realistic. For example, my code for treating others equitably is immutable; my code about bending rules to allow for creativity is…well…no rules. The personal code I'm suggesting is a secular career code, not a religious code, though your religious or spiritual beliefs certainly influence your behavior as a citizen. This is about your responsibility to yourself as a member of society, to others, and to the organization that is your work environment.

Reflecting on your personal code will aid in your career choices and decisions. Early leadership also involves drafting a code to work by. Like Portia, what are your own core values? What are the behavioral rules you live by? Think values, ethical principles, personal code of conduct. If you can identify your most important core values and understand why those values are important to you, it will help you navigate your way through your career journey.

Perhaps if you think of people you admire and identify what you most admire about them, that will help you pinpoint values. For example, what I admire about Sal Khan, founder of Khan Academy, is his commitment to providing free education to children. I admire choreographer Twyla Tharp's individualism, her independent creative thinking. I respect my husband for his unwavering integrity and commitment to medical care, among many other admirable values.

Identifying Your Core Values

You can break your core values into personal and business values. To make career choices consistent with personal standards—what you regard as important—identify your values.

List your top *five* core values, for example:

- Commitment to truth and honesty
- Self-respect and respecting others' personhood
- Compassion
- Integrity
- Upholding the truth
- Commitment to fairness and social justice
- Doing my personal best
- Being an upstanding citizen
- Economic security for all
- Commitment to diversity, equity, and inclusion
- Upholding the organization's standards and my own standards
- List other core values that are important to you:_____

_____

Let's keep articulating your values by answering the following questions:

• What are your reasons for these core values?
• What are your nonnegotiables? Think, "what I won't compromise."_____
• How do you want others to treat you?_____
• How do you treat others?_____
• How will your behavior be an example for others? Set you apart as a leader?_____

Here are values to consider and check off, though there are many others:

• Personal Achievement: performance, accomplishment, personal success via expertise, excellence, and distinction
• Truth: honesty, adherence to facts
• Justice: a belief in human equality with respect to social, political, and economic issues and affairs
• Fairness: impartial treatment, equity, which is related to justice
• Inclusion: being included in a group or structure; diversity in action
• Diversity: everyone deserves a seat at the organization's table and a voice in the conversation, which is related to inclusion
• Autonomy: freedom, agency, independence
• Respect: the quality of being esteemed for oneself as well as respect for others
• Compassion: sincere and empathic consciousness of others' distress together with a desire to alleviate it
• Fulfillment: satisfaction, contentment, happiness
• Stability: secureness, steadiness
• Tradition: cultural continuity in social attitudes, customs, and institutions
• Community (family or chosen family): building and sustaining relationships with others who hold similar values
• Culture: respect for one's own and for others' cultures

- Society: maintaining the voluntary association of individuals for a common end; working peacefully together toward a common goal of citizenhood
- Sustainability (Earth's conservation): sincere concern for protecting the planet and all of its creatures
- List other values that are important to you:_____.

Why recognize your values? Some careers or types of organizations respect certain values, and others do not. We've all read stories of corruption and greed in the news. If compassion is one of your top values, for instance, you might consider a career in social work or working for a nonprofit organization that serves people in any way. Or, if stability is a value, you might *not* select to work at a start-up or become an entrepreneur at the start of your career. If you value truth and justice, perhaps consider a career in journalism or human rights law.

Be the Hero of Your Own Story

You have trust in what you think. If you splinter yourself and try to please everyone, you can't. It's important to stay the course. I don't think I would have lasted this long if I'd listened to anyone. You have to listen somewhat and then put that to the side and know that what you do matters.

—Annie Leibovitz, portrait photographer[3]

The world is awash with prestige-TV antiheroes and prominent figures who are conspicuously lacking in heroic qualities. Although ultimately inscrutable, Machiavellian in character, greed and power seem to be what motivates many of these antiheroes.

When I read about tech titans, scammers, unscrupulous politicians, or people who trick investors using stupid, evil, and fraudulent ideas, I wonder why there are people who merely desire superficial goals—fame, power, or fortune—for their own sakes.

While there are some who agree with me, six in ten North American adults (60 percent) want to become billionaires one day, according to The Harris Poll's Americans and Billionaires Survey (conducted online within the U.S. by The Harris Poll in 2022, among a nationally representative sample of 1,989 U.S. adults).[4] Just ten years ago, a study found that a desire for fame solely for the sake of being famous was the most popular future goal among a group of 10- to 12-year-olds, overshadowing hopes for financial success, achievement, and a sense of community.[5] In a recent survey, 54 percent of Generation Z said they'd like to become an influencer, and 86 percent expressed interest in posting social media content for money.[6]

I'm a professor, so you can conclude that wealth and glory are not the motivating factors underlying my enduring career choice. What I did want and still do is an opportunity to form meaningful relationships with others, educate university students, educate readers through my writing, and find joy in my work. Of course I want to be successful; however, not without substance. My professional joy stems from my purpose as an educator in a professional academic degree program at a public university—to prepare my students for fulfilling and successful careers in design and advertising. When I see my former students enjoying successful careers, I feel gratified.

Back to heroes.

Any literature major can point to Joseph Campbell's *The Hero's Journey* as a must-read for understanding storytelling. Archetypal stories exist across cultures, communities, and time. But the content in *The Hero's Journey* isn't only for novelists or filmmakers—it's useful in determining what rings your bell career-wise.

You are the hero of your own professional story.

An archetype, from the Greek *archetypos* meaning original pattern, is a term popularized by the psychologist Carl Jung, which refers to a primordial image or character's role occurring consistently enough throughout literature and art as to be considered a universal concept.

It's interesting to understand how you relate to an *archetype* now.

Be the Hero of Your Own Story: Literary Archetypes

What you're looking for in the list below is if an archetype or a combination of archetypes is in sync with your personality traits or attitudes, behaviors, beliefs and values, ambitions, and desires.

- *The Hero*: Rises to meet any challenge, possesses courage and perseverance; saves the day
- *The Lover*: Romantic, passionate, guided by one's heart; builds relationships, enjoys intimacy
- *The Magician*: Alchemist, harnessed powers, omnipotent; helps people transform, grants wishes
- *The Outlaw*: Rebel, independent thinker, iconoclast, risk-taker; pushes boundaries
- *The Sage*: Wise, insightful, knowledgeable; helps people, provides practical information and guidance
- *The Innocent*: Hopeful, pure, sincere; trustworthy, holds strong to their values
- *The Creator*: Artistic, creative, ingenuous; steers cultural conversations
- *The Ruler*: Leader, exerts power over others; keeps order, omnipotent
- *The Caregiver*: Nurturing, supportive, service-oriented; serves the public good through education, health care, etc.
- *The Everyday Person*: Relatable, unpretentious, neighborly; fits in, regular, a buddy
- *The Citizen*: Believes in the humanity of everyone. Works toward the common good; advocate
- *The Explorer*: Seeker, adventurer; craves new experiences and journeys
- *The Warrior*: Soldier, rises to a challenge, assertive; achievement-oriented goals, nimble
- *The Jester*: Trickster, comic, disarming, insightful through humor, sassy, irreverent

You want to have humility, but you can't be shy to make clear to your supervisors, your leaders, whomever, what your aspiration is. Otherwise, people are going to just guess. Nobody, I promise you, cares more about your career than you do.

—Beth Ford, CEO of Land O'Lakes[7]

Interview: PJ Pereira

Figure 1.1 PJ Pereira, co-founder and creative chairman of Pereira & O'Dell

Photographer: Bronson Farr

PJ Pereira is an advertising and entertainment pioneer. He believes agencies must provide return not only for brands, but for the time consumers spend with the work. That balance is the ultimate challenge marketers face today.

PJ's credentials in content, digital, and advertising have made him one of the industry's most influential and respected creatives. He has been named to *Adweek*'s Creative 100 as Top Chief Creative Officer, *Ad Age*'s Creativity 50, and to the 4A's 100 People Who Make Advertising Great. Most recently PJ was named jury president of the inaugural AI discipline at the 2023 ADC Awards.

In 2023, under the name PJ Caldas, PJ will release a book (his fifth) titled, *The Girl from Wudang: A Novel About Artificial Intelligence, Martial Arts and Immorality*, about the unlikely combination of Artificial Intelligence (AI) and kung fu. Pereira is particularly drawn to the concept of an AI's influence in design and creativity, and he tries to engage this emerging technology in his own creative process whenever possible.

How and why did you decide on the advertising profession?

Ever since I was a kid, I knew I had a creative vein of some sort. I also knew that I didn't want to become an artist because if I were forced to create art all the time, so intensely, I might stop loving it. Therefore, I decided to learn more about technology and learn to program, which I enjoyed as well.

I thought, I know how to draw; I know how to write; I know how to program. So, I'll go into advertising because it's a way to best utilize all three skills. Advertising is a way to use my talent all the time without exhausting those talents.

You are one of the world's most influential and respected creatives and an advertising pioneer. Would you please offer some advice about thinking creatively?

It's really about thinking creatively in the long term. As I'm about to turn 50, I've been thinking more and more about how thinking creatively is not easy—it's mostly a matter of not becoming jaded so that you can stay free as a child, forever. There's nothing new in that, but the trick is how to think creatively for the duration. Being creative for a short time is easy. For the first seven years of life, you are—the advantage is to think creatively for the next seven and the next seven and the next seven and the next seven years. Forever.

The trick that I've found is to never have a single creative output, a single avenue for creative thinking. As a creative professional, you have to be creative on demand, which tends to burn you out.

Creativity is not a very efficient process. Logic is—where you go from point A to point B. And if you follow all the steps, you are going to get to point B. As a process, creativity is the opposite of logic. You know what A is and what B is; you try different things to see if you can get to B. Most of your creative ideas are not going to get you to B; however, eventually one of them will; and it's going to be different from processes based on logic, precisely because the creative process is not an efficient one.

The inefficiency of creativity is exactly why not everybody wants to employ it. That's one reason creativity gets killed at some point in life—we realize how inefficient it is, how challenging it is, and we stop trying. Logic is way more efficient, thus, it's a more predictable path. Thinking creatively involves uncertainty and might not always produce results. When some people realize this, they dispense with creative thinking. It's less about criticism, less about fear—it's about the practicality of it.

You also are a best-selling novelist. How do you manage both spheres of your professional and creative life?

People are baffled by how I have time for this. How do you have time? How do you do this? For me, it's not a matter of time, or of how I can manage; it's a necessity.

It's analogous to working out. If I don't work out, I'll die. If I don't work out, my body is going to be in so much pain from sitting in a chair for long periods of time. If I don't work out, I won't be able to think properly. Exercising is a discipline. It's similar to asking a basketball player why they do yoga; I need to stretch to have a longer career.

Having another creative output is like working out; it's not a matter of how I manage it, but a discipline that I need to extend my career. It's also important because it keeps my mental health in check.

Here's a practical example. When I present an idea that I love to a client, more often than not that idea gets killed—that's just the nature of the business. (People external to the advertising profession don't realize this.) For every awesome idea that gets produced, there have been twenty that get killed. If you're lucky, it's only twenty. And it's very likely that some ideas you truly love even more have been killed along the way, as well. That weighs very heavily on you. Having a second or third way to express your creativity helps you deal with that; especially because in advertising, creativity is a service. Ultimately, you're trying to solve someone's problem and you cannot mix the channels of self-expression and solving a problem. Sometimes the client is right. Sometimes what you're bringing is an incredible self-expression of what you're thinking or experiencing, but it's not what they need. When you have a second path for creative thinking, your work doesn't become the only way to express yourself. Thus, you're healthier and wiser.

How has your martial arts training benefited your mind and spirit?

I think it's the same thing—martial arts for me is a creative expression. It's another form of thinking. Even more than writing, it has to do with the way I identify myself. When I look in the mirror, I like to identify myself as a fighter, more than anything else. And that helps me.

In the best moments of advertising, I'm an advertising guy and a fighter. In the worst moments of advertising, I'm just a fighter. Having another identity gives you a backup for your emotional stability.

For example, when you go to a party and you're introduced to someone, you say, "I'm Robin; I'm a professor," or "I'm PJ; I'm an ad guy." The world has taught us that the thing directly after your name is your profession, which means that your identity gets associated with your craft. Therefore, any bump in your professional life is a strike to your self-esteem, is a strike to your sense of self-worth. Protecting that is very important.

When I look at myself in the mirror or when I introduce myself, I say, "I'm PJ; I'm a fighter," or "I'm PJ; I'm a writer," or "I'm PJ; I'm an ad guy." Having that choice alone adds fifteen more years to my career. On a bad day, I can say I'm a fighter. On a good day, I'm an ad guy.

As president of the ANDYs awards, you initiated a diversity mentorship program. Why is DEI important in advertising? How can others become advocates for DEI? Why is a mentor or sponsor important?

It's important in every profession but in advertising more than others because of the collective voice of advertising—that is, add up all the seconds that people worldwide listen to advertising. Advertising may lose only in strength and influence to entertainment.

We are responsible for what we say when we talk about anything. The things you say are influenced by who you are, and collectively we are too male, too white, and too young. We have to widen the professional collective to be more diverse and inclusive and responsible for what we say in mass media.

As a society, we impose responsibility on our footprint. For example, think about one factory's footprint. One factory owner could say, "The smoke emanating from my little chimney isn't going to change the climate; it's not going to cause hurricanes; it's not going to melt the polar cap." No; one factory might not, but collectively if everyone thinks that way, the environment will be a mess. The next generation will suffer.

We've finally agreed as a society that culture has a footprint. Little things that you might not notice individually collectively become a big problem. The divisiveness of culture today has been severely amplified by social media, the stickiness of social media, but it's also been caused by decades of advertising culture telling people that they need to be different from the rest of the world.

I think about the responsibility we have, the impact of what we're making, and the divisiveness and our obsession with pitting people against each other. For example, I know you wear Levi's because you're different from people who don't wear Levi's. The idea that your identity should be shaped not by what you have in common with others, but by how rebellious you are, how different you are from everyone else. That idea is small and harmless at level one, but it's very bad when it's repeated for decades by every brand in the world.

And that is just one problem when you have only one group of people running an entire industry with such voice power. You don't realize the harm you're causing.

What's the best career advice anyone has ever given to you?

The best career advice I received was from my uncle who told me that I was so creative that I should learn to program, as well. I replied that programming is not creative. He said, "Yes, it is. It's one of the most creative things that exist."

Programming helped me think about thinking, which is wonderful. I received that advice when I was 7 or 8 years old, and it shaped my entire life, my entire perception of what creativity is.

I am revisiting that moment now with AI. That's why I think AI is so important. AI is not just a creative tool, it is a new kind of computing. First was the big revolution that viewed computing as a series of instructions that we give to a machine, which it would then execute. Next, not only can the computer execute instructions, but it can trade instructions and data on a global level, which was the second computing revolution. We are going into a third phase, which is that computers not only follow instructions, not only share data on a global scale, but AI also makes decisions by itself.

If we learn and understand how to interact with computers that make decisions, we are set up for the new era of computing that is ahead of us in the next twenty years.

It's the difference between moving from riding a bike to riding a horse. You may not have as much control over a horse, but you have a beast that is way more powerful than you between your legs; with the flip side that the horse is going to make some decisions. You have to learn to communicate with it. Eventually you're going to tell a horse to turn to the right, and it turns to the left. That's similar to the conceptual AI situation we have to learn to deal with.

What's the best career advice you've ever given?

Understanding computing is an essential skill to understand the world. You don't need to be a computer scientist to understand computing. You need to understand computing in the same way you need to understand materials, entertainment, and information. Understanding computing is inescapable.

Notes

1   "The Best Career Advice for New Graduates," *Time*.com, https://time.com/charter/6188872/the-best-career-advice-for-new-graduates/

2   Stephanie Steinberg, "Money: Famous CEOs and Executives Share Their Best Career Advice," *U.S.News*.com, January 31, 2014. https://money.usnews.com/money/careers/slideshows/famous-ceos-and-executives-share-their-best-career-advice?slide=11

3   Rae Ann Fera, "Annie Leibovitz On Getting the Shot and the Future of Photography," *Fast Company*.com, June 28, 2013. https://www.fastcompany.com/2683295/annie-leibovitz-on-getting-the-shot-and-the-future-of-photography

4   "Americans and Billionaires Survey," *The Harris Poll*, 2022. https://theharrispoll.com/wp-content/uploads/2022/08/Americans-and-Billionaires-Survey-August-2022.pdf?utm_source=Newswire&utm_medium=PR&utm_content=america-loves-and-hates-its-billionaires-but-definitely-wants-them-to-21804699

5   Scott Barry Kaufman, "Beautiful Minds: Why Do You Want to be Famous?" *Scientific American*, September 4, 2013. https://blogs.scientificamerican.com/beautiful-minds/why-do-you-want-to-be-famous/

6 "The Influencer Report: Engaging Gen Z and Millennials," *Morning Consult*, 2022. https://morningconsult.com/influencer-report-engaging-gen-z-and-millennials/

7 Kelsey Doyle, "Beth Ford on Being the Champion of Your Own Career," Graduate School of Stanford Business.edu, July 7, 2021. https://www.gsb.stanford.edu/insights/beth-ford-being-champion-your-own-career

FINDING PURPOSE

DOI: 10.4324/9781003395034-3

Purpose is More Than a Job Description

When I asked Harry, my husband who is a physician with a PhD in Biology, why he left a career in genetics research behind to pursue a career in medicine, he replied, "Medicine always fascinated me. As a scientist, I didn't enjoy working alone in a lab; I wanted to interact with people."

People, indeed. Patients contact him at all hours for major or minor health issues. Harry works incredibly long hours at what I deem a very stressful career, making sure his patients are well. Yet, he's happy and fulfilled. I think about all the people he's kept healthy and alive. So...I asked him why he's happy being an endocrinologist when he has to work such long hours tending to patients and handling so much paperwork (think, insurance forms, letters to other physicians, etc.). Harry said, "I prefer a specialization that requires intellectual rigor, and I like keeping people healthy." Harry possesses a brilliant mind and could have easily enjoyed success in any number of careers. Many people would do well in a number of different careers that require similar aptitudes.

It's important to thoroughly reflect on how you can live a life imbued not just with the superficial trappings of success, but with purpose and joy in what you do many hours each day—starting now.

Follow Your North Star

Polaris, the North Star, is the brightest star in the constellation Ursa Minor, also known as the Little Dipper. It's called the North Star because its position in the night sky is almost directly over the North Pole. "Polaris is attention-getting, because unlike all the other stars in the sky, Polaris is in the same location every night from dusk to dawn, neither rising nor setting," according to astronomer and science communicator Dr. Richard Tresch Fienberg.[1] Due to its constant position in the sky, sailors have relied on the North Star as a navigational tool, as a guide.

Identifying your career's North Star is very useful. It could be your highest aspiration, immutable principles, great interest, or fervent belief. For example, you may be on a mission to fight for justice, protect workers' rights, improve cities' infrastructures, achieve your personal best, follow a passion for a discipline or sector, employ your creativity, or a combination thereof. Your North Star serves to keep you on course, a course aligned with your core principles and *élan vital*, which is your vital impulse.

However...

> One other note about the North Star is that it's a title that passes to different stars over time. Earth's axis of rotation wobbles over the course of about 26,000 years, the way a spinning top also wobbles as it spins. This causes the celestial pole to wander in a slow circle over the eons, sweeping past different stars... About 14,000 years ago, the celestial pole pointed toward the bright star Vega, and as it sweeps out its slow circle, it will again point to Vega in about 12,000 years.[2]

It won't take 12,000 years; however, your career's North Star is likely to change or morph, too. All of us are in the process of becoming who we are—personalities and desires are not static. Your future self might be quite different from your present self, as your present self quite likely is different from your much younger self. (Think back to when you were a child. Did you want to be a YouTuber, firefighter, professional athlete, or veterinarian? As a child, I wanted to be a professional dancer, astronomer, or fashion designer; I am none of those, although dancing is my avocation, and I still aspire to design a dress.) There may be constants; however, we continue to grow through acquired knowledge and experiences. Some beliefs might remain constant. For example, I have always advocated and worked for social justice; that belief is steadfast. However, my career path has changed a few times.

According to Henri Bergson (1859–1941), one of the most influential French philosophers of his time, the world is not composed of static objects isolated in empty space (which is far more complex than my elemental explanation). Instead, everything exists in duration—a continuous flow of time and space. Bergson influenced the

Cubists. The Cubist technique of depicting things simultaneously from different vantage points can be understood as presenting a Bergsonian conception of reality by rejecting a static single viewpoint and showing the object as constantly changing in the temporal and spatial flux. This is also indicated by the technique of depicting passage—breaking the boundaries between solid objects and surrounding space. I like to think of careers and North Stars as in temporal movement. We are always in the process of becoming who we are—never fixed.

For now, and likely a long while, your North Star helps to reorient you if you go off course, or it helps you stay on course to reach your intended destination.

What I wish I had known earlier in my career is stated so eloquently as follows:

> Be less of a Wonder Woman and more of a Woman of Wonder. Let curiosity be your compass, helping you discover what "lights you up." Seek diverse opportunities; it's just as informative to know what you don't care for or what you aren't great at, as it is to discover what gets you excited and where your natural talents lie. While no career will always be lollipops and rainbows, everyone deserves to ENJOY living out their life purpose. Just remember HOW your life's purpose plays out may change over time, so stay curious (and agile!).
> —Dr. Heather Frederick, author, podcast host, and change agent

Identifying Your Career's North Star: A Self-Assessment

To best identify your career's North Star, answer the following questions, which will serve to point you to true North and help you align your career goals with your personal code, vital life force, and discover what will resonate with your interests and expertise.

1. *Interests*: If you didn't have to earn a living, how would you spend your time? Your response should reveal your affinities, illuminating what type of pursuits and activities you find most engaging and rewarding.

Is it possible to connect your interests with your career, an optional career, or a side project?

What interests you most at work?

What interested you most in college or graduate school?

Check off a few of the following to examine your interests. I prefer a career with:

____Adventure: risk-taking work that is exciting

____Creativity: daily assignments or projects demanding idea generation, new products or services, creative problem-finding or problem-solving, or imagination skills

____Expressiveness: emotionally satisfying work

____Intellectual challenge: a career that requires great mental effort

____Theory: work that entails speculation and uncertainty

____Practicality: the use of things rather than theoretical; pragmatic work

____Discovery: the quest for new knowledge and continuous learning

____Diversity: meeting and working with lots of different people

____Collaboration: teamwork

____Philanthropy: work to promote the welfare of others; humanitarian work

____Service to society: work that in some part benefits the common good

____Applied research: opportunity to put research interests into practice

____Travel: opportunities to travel regularly or at least a few times a year

____Variety: working on different projects regularly

2. *Drive*: Knowing what type of work energizes you allows you to aim for a career that aligns with what drives you.

Ask yourself, What type of work satisfies my intellectual, creative, emotional, or humanitarian requisites? What aspects of work do I get excited about or look forward to? For instance, do you prefer to work on solo projects or on teams?

Do you prefer numbers-based or word-based work? Theoretical or practical problems to solve? Which experiences are or were stimulating or satisfying in the past, in college, or on an internship? Is helping others part of your aspirational career mix?

Check off a few of the following to examine your drive. I prefer a career with:

____Advancement: regular opportunities for work promotion or quick advancement

____Challenge: work with formidable (and engaging) projects and issues

____Novelty: constant new or unusual work; frequent change

____Personal satisfaction: work I enjoy or find pleasant or pleasurable

____Recognition: remarkable work accomplishments that are noticed and noted

____Wealth: work with more than sufficient income and rapid wealth escalation

____Expertise: work in my area of expertise or specialization

____Accomplishment: work that allows for personal satisfaction

____Independence: work that allows for autonomy

3. *Skills*: By identifying your skills, you'd best be able to realize your career options. Some skills are transferable from one work environment to another.

In the past, what have people, whether your instructors or managers, valued about your work, thinking, skills, or achievements?

Check off a few of the following to examine your skills. I prefer a career with an emphasis on:

____Technical skills

____Specialized skills

____Conceptual skills

List your current skills: _____

List skills you plan to acquire: _____

General skills:
____Research
____System development
____Presentation
____Time management, project management
____Leadership
____Negotiation
____Other:_____
Soft skills:
____Clear communication
____Creativity
____Problem solving
____Breaking down complex ideas
____Flexibility
____Adaptability
____Congeniality and cooperativeness (working well with others)
____Insight
____Idea generation
____Other:_____

4. *Environment*: Recognizing the kind of environment that allows you to thrive is very helpful. Ask yourself, Where do I want to live in the short- and long-term? What kind of organizational culture will allow me to thrive? In what type of culture would I best fit? Do I want to work full-time in one organization or be a temporary employee and move around frequently? Do I want to have a few part-time jobs (what we call a portfolio career) or work on a freelance basis? Is stability important to me? How competitive an environment can I withstand?

Check off a few of the following to examine the preferred environment and organizational culture. I prefer a career with:
____Ethics and values: work that aligns with my personal code
____Location: work in a preferred geographic location
____Attractiveness: work in an aesthetically pleasing environment

____Entrepreneurship: possibility for the development of my own work ideas or projects

____Structure: clearly defined work protocols

____Stability: probability of long-term employment, not volatile

____Portfolio career: Several part-time jobs or projects (vs. one full-time job)

____People contact: working directly with a large number of people

____Solitude: work with little contact with people

____Independence: a good amount of independent work and solo projects

____Knowledge: work with potential to learn, grow, and expand

____Work–Life balance: reasonable time demands for a professional-level career

____Authority: regular opportunities to lead and guide others and projects

____Pace:

    ____A fast-paced environment

    ____A slower pace of deadlines and lower-pressure environment

    ____Varied pace

5. *Purpose*: Identify the core purpose of your chosen career or work.

   Check off a few of the following to examine your preferences. Notice if the purpose is linked to your values or life goals.

   ____I am connected to something bigger than myself.

   ____My work matters; I feel useful.

   ____My work matters to individuals and/or society.

   ____I want to contribute to my discipline or move it forward.

   ____I use my talent.

   ____I use my skills.

   ____I find this type of work enjoyable or rewarding for a number of reasons.

The Shape of You

How do you know what you want in a career? How do you know what you will find fulfilling? These categories should serve as a good starting point to help you determine where you're at.

- Activities that you enjoy:_____
- Educational experiences that have shaped your thinking:_____
- Work or events that have shaped your thinking:_____
- Others who have influenced your thinking:_____
- Experiences that have impacted your interests:_____
- Skills you have developed:_____
- Skills you want to develop (be specific):_____
- Transferable skills to other careers or disciplines:_____

Your Career's North Star Worksheet

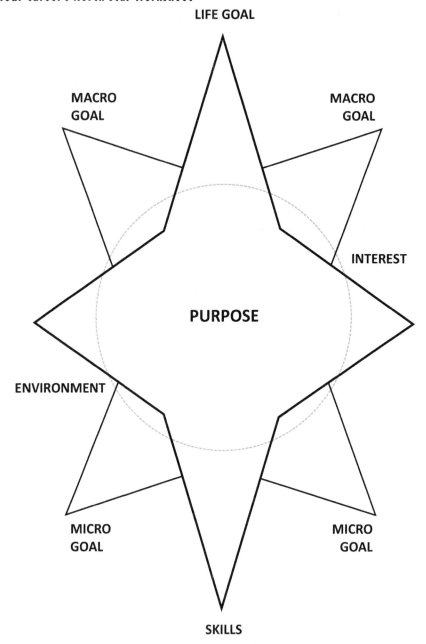

Figure 2.1 Diagram of a North Star. Write your responses inside the star.
Illustration: Patrycja Sliwowska

A Career Led by Interests and Experiences

You want to thrive. Whether you conduct an interest assessment or follow your known interests, identifying your interests takes you down a well-suited path. You also can identify interests along the way through experiences. An interest assessment asks you to check off categories and activities that interest you the most, with categories such as: Practical (think, pilot or forest ranger), Investigative (think, historian or scientist), Artistic (think, writer or filmmaker), Social (think, counselor or teacher), Enterprising (think, entrepreneur, influencer, or stock trader), or Analytical (think, accounting or editing).

To align your interests with a career, imagine a potential employer asking you, "What interests you most about this job?"

> **Have a direction, but it doesn't have to be the right one (or the only one).**
>
> You have to have one; otherwise, things just don't work right. But feel free to take scenic routes, go off-road, follow detours, and if you find a better direction, then take that one. In college, I started off as a math major, then architecture/engineering, and finally psychology. Off to grad school, clinical internships and post-docs and practicing. But today, I'm happily doing nothing remotely close to what I envisioned at 22, nevertheless I'm glad it came about the way it did. I feel much more enriched as a result. Rarely is there a learning experience (no matter the field) that would not be a help to who you are and what you do. Sometimes a detour is because the bridge is out... Regardless of a varying trajectory, keep in mind that if you doubt how good your work is, then you are probably doing it right—whatever it is.—Dr. Chris E. Stout, founding director, Center for Global Initiatives[3]

Portfolio Career

Doing one thing doesn't suit some people who prefer variety. A portfolio career encompasses multiple part-time jobs, income-producing projects, or freelance work as opposed to having one full-time job. Having multiple streams of income from a variety of sources and endeavors fulfills some professionals' need for flexibility and variety or employing various skills and expertise.

For those who have *transferable* skills, or skills that can be used in more than one career, the benefits of a portfolio career include opportunities to work in multiple sectors or industries. Experience across industries allows people to diversify, switch fields, cultivate experiences, as well as learn what best fits their long-term plan. If you prefer to compose a career, consider how your skills, interests, experience, and expertise can be applied across disciplines or sectors.

Vital Life Force

In his book *Creative Evolution* (1907), Bergson exalts the concept of a creative force that he called *élan vital*, which he believed distinguishes heroic individuals among the populace. If we adopt Bergson's *élan vital* for our own purpose, ask,

• What distinguishes you from your peers?
• What work energizes you?
• Why do you want to do a certain type of work?

Intention

Think about the overall relevance and significance of your career, of what would intensify or enrich it. Ask,

• What impact do you hope your work will have?
• What is the legacy you aspire to leave as a professional or as a leader?
• Which of your expertise, hard or soft skills, do professional colleagues appreciate about you?

Self-Inventory

More than ever, people switch careers, whether it's moving from one industry to another or within a sector. The reasons for change might include work–life balance, a progressive corporate culture, newly acquired academic degrees or continuing education, or the desire for greater flexibility.[4]

Either way, that's where goals (the end toward which your effort is directed, what you want to achieve), ambitions (a desire for rank, fame, or power), or intentions (a determination to act) come into your plan. You could play it by ear; however, establishing goals is an obvious step to building a strong foundation (and timeline) for the most satisfying career possible.

In the following chapters, we'll explore goals and how they can shape your career.

Interview: Anita Schjøll Abildgaard

Anita Schjøll Abildgaard is CEO and co-founder at Iris.ai—a semifinalist in the AI for Good XPRIZE 2020 and a recipient of the EIC Accelerator 2023. She is also faculty in AI at Singularity University and the Re:Humanize Institute. She was included among the world's top 50 women in tech by *Forbes* in 2018.

Figure 2.2 Anita Schjøll Abildgaard, CEO and co-founder of Iris.ai

Photography: Iris.ai

In the past decade, her career has spanned ten industries including developing an E-learning tool in Silicon Valley, reducing energy consumption in the process industry, facilitating a solar light business in Kenya, and trying to disrupt the recruitment industry. She also went to six universities along the way. And she built a race car.

According to something you've said, you've never had what you refer to as "a real job." Iris.ai is your fourth own start-up. What advice would you give someone who would also prefer to not have a conventional job?

Back in 2013, I was studying for a master's degree in Entrepreneurship and Business Design. It was a practical degree, where we started companies as part of our final year. I'd already spent a couple of years working for a start-up in Silicon Valley and started my first little company prior to that. Months away from graduation, a very large proportion of my classmates started obsessing about high-end exclusive trainee program applications—with the likes of McKinsey and other high-end, high-paid management consultancies. I started wondering if I should be contemplating these things as well, since everyone was so preoccupied with them. There was a sentiment of a "career ladder" one had to climb, and I was wondering if I had missed the memo. We had access to a career coach through school, so I asked her point blank whether I had missed something, and I should jump on this and start applying to things. She gave me the best career advice I ever got—honestly, it might be the only one I've ever taken—which is that "your career is not a ladder to be climbed. It is simply the sum of everything you've done up until now." I had already gotten to do a lot of cool and unique things, learned so much, and with her statement I left behind any notion of a particular path to follow.

How did you determine your career path and purpose?

I never quite did. As in, there has never been a clear plan to what I do. I've always known that I want what I do to have meaning; that what I work on, in some small or large way, might mean something real to someone. That what I do with my time here on this planet matters. That's been a guiding principle—that, together with wanting to learn as much as possible on the way. I absolutely love soaking up new information and understanding more of the world. And finally, I want to have fun. It doesn't mean I have to enjoy every single moment, because a lot of what I do is very hard. Running a start-up comes with a lot of highs and lows, and there have definitely been some rough patches with my current (and past) company where I question whether it's worth it to keep going. So, then it comes to whether I still believe that what I do has meaning, and whether I am still learning. As much time as we humans spend at work, it's always been vital to me that my days are filled with things that are challenging, difficult, and enjoyable.

Finally, a lot of the brilliant opportunities that have shown up in my path may seem like pure chance. To a certain degree they are, but one thing I've always done is say "yes," which has been helpful. For example, in the first year at my master's degree in 2011, we were asked if someone from our class could help out at an Entrepreneurship conference (which we would not be invited to until we were alumni). I volunteered, even though there was nothing really "in it for me" other than serving coffee to some people for an afternoon. But, the following year I was asked to join the organizing committee and ended up being toastmaster, and eventually organizer of the full event the year after that, and through all that I met some people who introduced me to some other people who I eventually started my next company with. One of them was accepted into Singularity University in 2014 and told me I absolutely had to apply in 2015 and wrote me the best recommendation letter I have ever seen in my life, which got me into the Singularity GSP summer school on a scholarship from Google. I do firmly believe that a genuine desire to be helpful and say yes to things, even if I don't see a clear direct benefit, has led to so many opportunities in my life.

Is creative thinking or imagination necessary for careers such as yours? Why?

I do believe creativity is a necessity to build innovative companies, for sure—being a visionary, thinking outside the box, and dreaming big. However, there's also a need for systematic thinking, analysis, financial management, and a range of other skills that do not necessarily require full-blown creativity. At Iris.ai, we are today a trio of co-founders who work very well together and have highly complementary skills—from technology understanding via storytelling to financial and strategic analysis. That is what has made the company a success so far, not solely a vivid imagination.

How did you become interested in Artificial Intelligence (AI) and what did you do to make it a career path?

When attending GSP15 at Singularity University, we were challenged to form teams around a problem and find ideas for how to solve it—ideas that would positively impact the lives of a billion people in a decade. We formed a team, quickly discovered our joint obsession with making scientific knowledge more accessible, and as we dove into potential ways that problem could be solved, we realized Artificial Intelligence was a must in that undertaking. So, I didn't fall in love with a technology to go looking for a problem to solve with it; I fell in love with a problem, and the technology became a necessity. In the past I had worked on highly technical and mathematical projects, but this was my first venture into AI. My love for learning complex things, and figuring out ways to communicate it in understandable terms depending on the audience, helped me a lot in becoming someone people would ask to talk about this emerging technology. Sometimes labeled an "expert," I think I just learn fast and can re-explain it in ways that make it understandable. If I have a superpower, this is probably it; and I get to use it a lot in my work life and truly enjoy it.

Iris.ai is focused on training Artificial Intelligence to tackle scientific information and make it digestible for researchers. How will this mission impact science and make Research & Development better?

Our ultimate goal is simple enough: we want everyone who has a big problem to solve to be able to have all the scientific information about the problem and potential solutions at their fingertips, so they can actually solve the problem rather than just trying to find information about it. We're living in a world where we have an unprecedented amount of scientific knowledge published on a daily basis, but to solve humanity's biggest problems, we need full interdisciplinary connections—something that is becoming increasingly difficult with the sheer volume of publications. So, we're building an AI system that can do this for us.

Notes

1 Patrick J. Kiger, "Why Is the North Star So Stellarly Important?" *Howstuffworks*.com, updated February 5, 2021. https://science.howstuffworks.com/north-star.htm
2 Preston Dyches, "What is the North Star and How Do You Find It?" Solarsystem.Nasa.gov, July 28, 2021. https://solarsystem.nasa.gov/news/1944/what-is-the-north-star-and-how-do-you-find-it/
3 Chris E. Stout, "Dear Graduates, Now Is the Time to Mess Up," LinkedIn.com, May 27, 2014. https://www.linkedin.com/pulse/20140527114626-3055695-if-i-were-22-now-is-the-time-to-mess-up/
4 Peter Laurie, "Topics/Workforce: 5 Reasons People Are Changing Careers More Than Ever Before," USChamber.com, December 14, 2021. https://www.uschamber.com/workforce/5-reasons-people-are-changing-careers-more-than-ever-before

SETTING YOUR GOALS

03

DOI: 10.4324/9781003395034-4

What's Life Got to Do with It?

How you frame your life goals also frames your career, endeavors, and relationships with others.

Life goals are the grand ones—the pot-of-gold-at-the-end-of-the-rainbow ones. For example, someone's life goal might be practicing human rights law or playing the cello for a symphony orchestra, or someone might want to be both a human rights attorney and a performing musician, or be a human rights attorney as well as care for a big family. To achieve a life goal, you need to plan incremental goals to get you where you want to be.

Of course, some people have rather broad life goals, such as being famous or rich.

You'll notice I called the grand one a "life goal" and not a "career goal," even though this book is dedicated to career guidance. Your life goal very likely also includes family, friends, romantic partners, hobbies, leisure, community affiliations, charitable work, and your overall well-being. Career is a huge one nested within your life goal.

Framing career goals with purpose can lead to attaining a fulfilling life goal.

What's your life goal, as of now? Let's figure it out, if you haven't already.

- In the future, I would like to be able to tell my family and friends that I accomplished the following:_____
_____

- If you were a wise friend or your favorite professor, what advice regarding a life's goal would you offer to yourself?
_____

- If you knew there was indeed a pot of gold (or however you define success) at the end of your life goal's rainbow, what would you pursue?_____

Framing Your Career Goals

Basically, there are two types of career goals that you set for yourself: macro-goals and micro-goals (or concurrent goals). To attain what you desire and feel fulfilled in any role, you need to set and achieve both types of goals.

Career macro-goals are often longer term and generally more substantial. Think of your macro-goal as your "North Star" guiding your career. Career micro-goals are smaller, actionable goals that you can pursue in tandem with your macro-goal. It makes sense to first consider and set your macro-goal, and then work backward setting your micro-goals to help you reach your bigger or macro-career goals.

A macro-goal can be a number of major target plans: finding a career that best matches your interests, mastering your discipline, becoming a thought leader in your field, making an impact in your discipline or on the world at large, expanding your knowledge through higher education or continuing education, improving the quality of life of others, or even finding a job that challenges you to grow.

> I always did something that I was a little not ready to do. I think that is how you grow. When there's a moment of "Wow, I'm not so sure that I can do this," and you push through those moments, it's then that you have a breakthrough. Sometimes that's a sign that something really great is about to happen. You're about to grow and learn a lot more about yourself.
> —Marissa Mayer, former president and CEO of Yahoo and founder of tech incubator Lumi Labs

If you're unsure of what macro-goal to set or what would make the most sense, a good way to start is to figure out what you *don't* want to pursue. Misalignment of one's goals and career can be the source of not being fulfilled in your job. Think of this as your "What I Don't Want" assessment.

Answer the following seven questions:

- **Which careers do *not* suit my personality, interests, or expertise?** For instance, if you're a people person, a career without collaboration or direct interaction with co-workers or external stakeholders is likely *not* best suited for you. Or if your expertise or interests lie in the digital space and you have to spend a good deal of your time in-person with customers, well, this is probably *not* a good fit either.

- **Which roles or functions do I *not* want to perform?** Within a general job category, for example, would you *not* want to perform essential support, operational and technical, supervisory or managerial roles, sales, cross-functional, or other professional roles?

- **What work–life balance conditions would *not* work for me?** What would *not* be a sustainable work–life balance for you? Working extremely long hours? Being on call? Work that doesn't drain you so that you have some energy left when you get home?

- **What am I *not* willing to sacrifice?** Many professional occupations involve sacrifice of some kind. For example, it's good to know beforehand if you would *not* be willing to sacrifice your weekends or nights to work for a long period, or sacrifice time with family due to work travel. (Though it may be hard to avoid these sacrifices during the early career years or in a number of types of careers.)

- **To determine whether I will "fit in," what kind of company culture would I *not* thrive in?** The company's culture often determines if you would or would *not* fit in. Think, competitive, global, very high management expectations, many hours beyond the conventional workday, lack of world-class talent, fast-paced environment, innovative, performance-based or traditional, or top-down ideas.

- **What type of projects do I *not* enjoy working on?** Think about whether you would *not* find fulfillment in writing reports, working in a lab environment, working on cross-disciplinary or cross-country projects, doing administrative work, planning events, performing systems installations, working on year-long projects, and so on. (For example, in my university faculty role, I also can elect to be an administrator of an academic program, but I don't relish that; I much prefer teaching.)

- **What would make me feel down at the end of the day?** There are all types of stressors. For example, determine if any of the following would cause you undue stress: multitasking, how management judges your performance, non-inclusive teams, lack of faith in the work you're doing, competitive co-workers, a long commute, remote work, poor remuneration, not being intellectually challenged, being overwhelmed with work, and so on.

While these questions may seem broad, they can help you identify *red flags* to avoid as you pursue your next role or work to improve your current situation—and ultimately give you insights that will move you closer to your macro-goal. For example, maybe you discover that you don't want to perform in a leadership or management role, or you don't want to work in a place that doesn't offer flexible, hybrid, or remote work arrangements. Knowing this, and given your current expertise and job, are you on the right path?

Follow up by asking yourself:

- What would I like to work on over the next year or two?
- What are my personal strengths? Which ones should I capitalize on? What do I need to improve?
- What would I want my work situation to look like at the end of this time period?
- Do I need to advance my current career or change careers to do this?
- What needs to be done, in what order, and by when?

Knowing what you don't want, and now a little more about what you do, *work backward* by setting a few micro-goals to help you get there. For example, let's pretend that upon completing this exercise, someone realizes that they want to be working as a copywriter in an advertising agency two years down the line. This person currently works as a personal assistant to an advertising creative director. What can they do?

They can set a couple of micro-goals to help them shift their career path. They could prepare a portfolio of work for entry into the creative side of the advertising profession. Or they could use their current writing skills and experience in the agency to transition into a junior role as a copywriter, or ask their supervisor, the creative director, if they can work on a pro-bono assignment or any client assignment. Doing any one of these would allow them to learn more about copywriting and the creative side of the business, while developing insider knowledge. Another micro-goal could be investing in an online or in-person (if available) copywriting course or workshop. They also could request "informational interviews" with advertising copywriters to find out more about that career. An *informational interview* is a short meeting between someone who wants to investigate a career and a person working in that career, with the goal to find out more about a job that might interest and suit you.

> Talent, on its own, can never replace clear goals, a plan, and hard work.
> —Gabriel Fuentes, director, Design Action Studio for Research, Architecture, and Urbanism, and assistant professor of Architecture, Kean University

Set Macro- and Micro-goals

Break your goals down into macro- and micro-goals. Using a simple tree map to set a macro-goal and organize or classify micro-goals beneath the macro-goal is easy and helpful. When you actually visualize your goals, it aids organizing them in a hierarchical order.

To get going, even if you're unsure of your macro-goal right now, select one that is best suited to your life goal.

Mapping your goals:

- Write your macro-goal at the top of the page.
- Under the macro-goal, list three micro-goals that would help you achieve your macro-goal.
- In hierarchical order, number the micro-goals that are concurrent with your macro-goal.

A couple of micro-goals could be concurrent as well. For instance, gaining a new skill could be concurrent with arranging informational interviews with potential mentors and industry leaders or networking or attending leadership training workshops. Whereas earning an advanced degree is best as a single goal, due to its inherent demands on your time and resources.

For example, let's say someone wants to work in the communications industry, specifically public relations, shaping public and intercorporate images. The Public Relations Society of America (PRSA) defines this career as follows, "Public relations is a strategic communication process that builds mutually beneficial relationships between organizations and their publics."[1] This career requires good writing and verbal communication skills as well as the ability to influence people. It also likely requires a university degree, and might require crafting press releases and responses (in a hurry), putting out fires for clients, multitasking, being a nimble thinker, gracefully handling and responding to clients, working for more than one client at a time, planning events or press conferences, and much more.

If this person holds a university degree, they can build on their communication skills, which might entail setting a micro-goal of taking a continuing education course in writing for business or for social media or earning a specialized certificate. Another micro-goal could be taking an assertiveness training course (which I highly recommend for everyone). Another micro-goal might be to learn how to generate original ideas, which is often required in a career with a dynamic and unpredictable landscape. If this individual has no experience in public relations, finding a paid internship, an entry-level job, or a mentor would set them in the right direction.

When you think about the outcomes of your goals, rather than see each as an end result, try to focus on accomplishing one that leads to the next. And if one doesn't work out, you have others to work on. There are different types of micro-goals.

Process goals are the actions you take and activities you participate in to move you ahead and toward a bigger goal. These help guide your path, as well. If we think about the aspiring copywriter, they could set a process goal of working on their portfolio every weekend or free-writing at lunchtime.

Practical and finite goals are micro-goals that you can achieve in a limited amount of time and with a fixed amount of resources, for example, taking a six-week copywriting or management training course.

Growth goals are about growing overall and replenishing your knowledge base, for example, continuously taking courses in a variety of disciplines, learning a new language, getting better at math or reading, and so on.

Stretch goals are those that challenge you, ones that make greater demands but offer potentially greater rewards.

Discovery goals are about exploring, finding out more about what might interest you the most.

Performance goals are micro-goals you set to improve the quality or speed of your performance at work or in your field of study, productivity (think, improving sales to obtain a promotion), or, for example, setting a numeric target or a time to achieve the goal.

Interview: Dr. Carl M. Truesdale

Figure 3.1 Dr. Carl M. Truesdale, Beverly Hills Board Certified facial plastic and reconstructive surgeon

Photographer: Eric Williams

Dr. Carl M. Truesdale is a Beverly Hills Board Certified facial plastic and reconstructive surgeon. His advanced knowledge of facial anatomy and his artist's eye enable him to deliver natural-looking results for all surgical and non-surgical procedures. He truly sees his facial plastic surgery practice as one of his main purposes on Earth!

Dr. Truesdale's lifelong passions for medicine, culture, and the arts led him to double major in Biology and Spanish at Morehouse College, where he graduated summa cum laude. He then earned his M.D. at Perelman School of Medicine at the University of Pennsylvania, one of the top 3 medical schools in the United States.

Dr. Truesdale completed five years of specialized surgery training in Otolaryngology – Head and Neck Surgery at the top-ranked University of Michigan. During residency, he completed a surgical mission to Ghana where he taught surgical techniques, lectured, and performed life-saving procedures.

Dr. Truesdale continued his training by specializing in facial plastic surgery, and completed a facial plastic surgery fellowship in Beverly Hills, California. He began building his facial plastic surgery practice as a fellow, and decided to plant roots in the Los Angeles area for the long term.

Dr. Truesdale is an active member of the American Academy of Facial Plastic and Reconstructive Surgery and the American Academy of Otolaryngology – Head and Neck Surgery. He has authored and presented multiple peer-reviewed papers at national meetings.

Dr. Truesdale maintains his commitment to language and the arts and is described as a "modern-day renaissance man," with talents not only as a skillful surgeon but also as a portrait artist, musician, and pilot.

How did your lifelong passions for medicine, culture, and the arts lead you to medicine and specifically to facial plastic surgery?

When I look back on my life's journey, it all seems to have led me here. I grew up in a small town in Upstate New York. My dad is a scientist, a PhD. So, I always grew up with having science around, and my mom is a creative, she's an artistic woman, an artist herself. I always had those two kinds of aspects—the science and the artistic side.

When I was very young, around the age of 10, I had a baby brother who unfortunately passed away from Trisomy 13. When he passed, I found myself trying to figure out answers. What happened to him? What's going on? We had a home study that included a medical encyclopedia; I remember reading about his condition, which was only a short paragraph. But I realized this entire book was filled with other conditions. It was at that moment that I decided I wanted to become a doctor. I did everything I could to accomplish that goal.

Transitioning through school, I had a lot of academic achievements. By the time I got to medical school at the University of Pennsylvania, I figured out that I wanted to become a surgeon because I love working with my hands; there are a lot of things that I like to do with my hands. I started researching surgical subspecialties, one of which is head and neck surgery–otolaryngology; I fell in love with this specialty, taking care of everything above the shoulder. One part of that subspecialty is facial plastic and reconstructive surgery. My background as a portrait artist, as a scientist, and as someone who wanted to take care of people melded. Now I am a facial plastic and reconstructive surgeon.

You've said that you see your facial plastic surgery practice as one of your purposes on Earth. Please tell us about defining your purpose or how you found your purpose.

We can become very philosophical here.

I think we all have something that we're good at, that we have a penchant towards. If you want to, think about the idea that we're all working together, all waves floating in the universe. For me, my harmony, the thing that gets me going is art and creating, and helping people. My career allows me to do that. I view what I do through medicine as an extension of art. The human form is my canvas, in particular, the face. I get to help people work through their own journey by helping them change things they would like to change with their appearance. This has satisfied a lot of components of who I am—my creativity and my desire to help people but also other things; the analytical side, running a business, leading a team, learning constantly—all of those things are skills you have to keep sharpening in this job. I feel very satisfied and lose myself while doing surgery sometimes. There's the concept of a flow state; I'm really in my flow state, whether I'm playing music or doing a ten-hour surgery.

It takes great commitment and time to pursue a career in medicine. Would you please tell us about how you set your life goal and macro-goals?

It all started way back when I was 10, but at that age you really don't know about the path. You learn more as you grow. I've always been very inquisitive and try to seek out answers to my questions.

I knew I needed to be a good student. I knew I needed to do well in science and that's pretty much all I knew when I was 10. When I got to middle school and then high school, I became much more laser-focused. I knew that I needed to take high-level biology and chemistry classes and do some research or extracurriculars that would make my application good for a university application as a stepping stone to get to medical school, residency, and fellowships.

What I like to do is break down large goals into the fundamental steps needed to accomplish them. Then at the highest level try to condense those learnings down and get those tasks completed. By the time I graduated high school, I had 26 college credits to transfer to college so that I was able to double major in biology and Spanish and advance quickly. When I was in college, I had multiple published papers, a patent, medical research, I had volunteered, participated in student government, and graduated summa cum laude. I did everything necessary to secure admission into an Ivy League medical school, ensuring that no opportunities or doors remained closed. When I got to medical school, I did an extra year of research; I did very well in my academic studies, in all of the courses; published research; I did all of the things I needed to do so that I could get into the best residency program, which was at the University of Michigan—so that I could get the best surgical training to become the kind of surgeon I wanted to be. And that just continues.

I break down each large goal into the smaller fundamental goals trying to achieve them at the highest level so that no opportunity or door is shut.

You've generously created a foundation, a nonprofit to help those who cannot afford corrective surgery, with services to military veterans, domestic abuse survivors, victims of bullying, and others. Why is service to others important to you?

I think it ultimately comes down to how I was raised—to my parents—if you really dig in. And it's been reinforced across my life. At Morehouse College, there's the idea that we stand on the shoulders of the people who come before us. We're trying to reach a crown that we will never grow tall enough to reach. The people who come after us stand on our shoulders. It's that kind of idea—that if we're all not moving forward, and we're not nice and good people on this Earth together, then we're really not accomplishing anything.

I made a definitive decision to become a facial plastic and reconstructive surgeon in residency. In residency, I learned everything from ear surgery, cochlear implants, head and neck cancer surgery, voice surgery, sleep surgery—all of these skills that I have. I chose to do mostly cosmetic work, but there's a lot of facial plastic, cosmetic, and reconstruction; in a lot of what I do day to day, I'm not able to exercise that larger skill set. To balance those things, I wanted to be able to give back and help people who may be involved in trauma—anything from burns to gunshot wounds, to domestic abuse, to cleft lip and palate, to people who don't like the way they look and they just can't afford services. It's a way to give back using the skill set that I learned over many years of training.

Is there something or some personal trait that you feel is most responsible for your success? What kind of skills does it take to become successful and an inspiring leader?

There are probably a lot of traits, but I'll say it's confidence, which was instilled in me as a child. There were no limits that my parents put on me. So, if I thought I could fly, well, they'd let me find out that I can't fly but put down the mattresses so I could jump off the stairs. And that just continued. That confidence was something that allowed me to not put limits on what I thought I could achieve. Whether that's to start a private practice in the most competitive place in the world or start a business or whatever it may be, I feel very confident to bet on myself, to make that investment in myself. And I'm always trying to improve in every aspect of my life and learn.

Those three things: confidence, not putting limits on what I could achieve, and investing in myself have served me well.

You've said, the most successful people have a learner's mindset. Would you elaborate please?

Anyone can do an action and fail. You can either learn from other people's failures or you can fail yourself, but you have to do the learn; and, then you have to execute.

You need a vision, which identifies whatever the thing is that you're trying to do. You might fail. But if you learn, or before you even have a chance to fail, you can learn from others, then you can achieve.

Every year, outside of medicine or business, I try to learn something new and interesting, whether it's flying a plane, playing guitar, or whatever it might be, I'm always trying to learn. Those things learned carry forward in the day-to-day. On my way to work this morning, I was listening to podcasts about entrepreneurship, public relations, marketing, running an effective team, and financing. Looking at the different components of my day-to-day so that I'm constantly learning; that's what bumps you up at every level.

What's the best career advice anyone has ever given to you?

Specifically, the best investment you can make is in yourself. That can be translated in a lot of different ways, but if you don't put the investment in, then you won't reap the benefit.

Everyone has their own lane. If you want to be a surgeon, you need to put the investment into going to medical school and all the hours, and the blood, sweat, and tears to make that happen. If you want to be an entrepreneur, you have to make the investment in learning the business, breaking it down, and getting better. If you don't take any risks, in particular on yourself, then you can't achieve anything.

What's the best career advice you've ever given?

I have a lot of people that I mentor. I can speak globally about that. However, in particular, there was a medical student I was mentoring who wanted to go into otolaryngology. He was discouraged by his test scores. Otolaryngology, head and neck surgery, is a very competitive specialty; you really need very strong Step 1 scores, letters of recommendation, and all of the above. He was a decent medical student, but he didn't have good research or a very strong Step 1 score, which is one of the big things residencies look at.

So, we did a very hard, deep look into his position and I counseled him, "Hey, you really need to bolster your application in some ways." He then made the decision to take an extra year of research. Going forward, he's doing well; he's in residency, and we were able to get him through. The impact can be felt on an individual level or on a global level.

A lot of times when I'm mentoring people in terms of their career, I'm telling them the basic things: find your path, think through it, don't give up, it's a long road, it's hard, you're going to be exhausted. Anyone can say that, but it probably makes a huge impact on everyone. Specifically, I highlighted this one person's example because I think it changed the trajectory of their entire life.

Why do you mentor?

I love teaching. I love the impact. I have had a lot of great teachers in my life. It feels good. I have a lot to share.

Why do we do anything? We probably get something back from it. And I get back more than my mentees probably get. When you see the person who is trying to get into medical school and you walk them through all of the different things they need to do, and then they get into medical school, it feels like you got into medical school again. It just feels really good.

Note

1   "Public Relations Defined: A Modern Definition For The New Era Of Public Relations," *PRSA*.org, April 11, 2012. http://prdefinition. prsa.org/

GOALS

Which overarching macro-goal holds the highest priority for you at this moment? That's the goal you'll be focusing on in this worksheet.

Have you determined your micro-goal(s)? What are the three most critical microgoals that will support your macro-goal?

THE FUNCTION OF GOALS

04

DOI: 10.4324/9781003395034-5

The Function of Goals

Hoping doesn't get you where you want to go. Setting and carrying out proactive professional goals do. Similarly, a wish is not a plan. Let's take "hope" and "wish" out of our professional vocabulary. Actions work much better. Recognize the steps, rewards, and sacrifices necessary to achieve your goals.

In the previous chapter, Dr. Carl M. Truesdale explained, "I break down each large goal into the smaller fundamental goals trying to achieve them at the highest level so that no opportunity or door is shut." For many people goals fulfill several functions:

- *Alignment*: All macro- and micro-goals should align with your life goal intention.
- *Hierarchy*: Arrange all goals in a hierarchy of importance and time/energy/demands; prioritize your activities, which should be orchestrated to achieve your life goal. (Although some micro-goals are terrific endeavors no matter what, for instance, a writing or personal finance course or assertiveness training.)
- *Executive function*: Planning and managing your resources (time, money, energy) to achieve your life goal is vital to growth.
- *Furtherance*: Making progress toward achieving your life goal. Focus on continuation and growth.
- *Getting from A to B*: The key function of establishing macro- and micro-goals is to get you to where you want to be, often step-by-step.
- *Motivation*: Having a challenging goal motivates you, according to the research by Dr. Edwin Locke and Dr. Gary Latham, in *New Developments in Goal Setting and Task Performance*, whose interest lies in understanding work motivation.[1] Results from a review of laboratory and field studies on the effects of goal setting on performance showed that in 90 percent of the cases, having specific and

challenging goals led to higher performance than easy goals or no goals.[2]

To make goals easier to recognize and monitor, they should be "concrete and specific," according to Dan Ariely, author of *Predictably Irrational: The Hidden Forces That Shape Our Decisions*.[3]

George T. Doran devised and published the S.M.A.R.T. goals and objectives system for managers in his 1981 article, "There's a S.M.A.R.T. Way to Write Management's Goals and Objectives"; many managers as well as other individuals (as opposed to only managers in organizational settings) find it very useful for setting professional goals and assessing what they plan to do. The S.M.A.R.T. acronym stands for:

Specific: Target a specific area for improvement.
Measurable: Quantify or at least suggest an indicator of progress.
Achievable: Specify who will do it (in an organization).
Relevant: State what results can realistically be achieved, given available resources.
Timely: Specify when the result(s) can be shared.[4]

People have created variations on Doran's system. One reason to use such a system, aside from efficacy, is for its objectivity. You can easily amend it or pull what works for you from it; for example, this might work best for any early career:

- *Attainable*: Which actions do you need to take to achieve what you want?
- *Relevant*: How will this action or goal be relevant to your overall growth, success, and career journey? Very importantly, why do you think this goal is important? How will it get you where you want to be?
- *Practical*: How realistic is this goal in terms of time, resources (your energy, money [loans, liquid funds, amount],

materials, assistance), and work–life balance? However, don't be so practical that you eliminate what might appear to be risks. Playing it safe often doesn't lead to growth.

- *Obstacles*: What is standing between you and achieving your goals—time, money, agency, commitments, access? How can you overcome one or more of these?
- *Results*: The XYZ formula comes from Laszlo Bock, co-founder of Humu and Gretel.ai, former Google chief human resources officer, and author of *Work Rules!*

The XYZ formula means, "Accomplished X, as measured by Y, by doing Z." Bock writes, "In other words, start with an active verb, numerically measure what you accomplished, provide a baseline for comparison, and detail what you did to achieve your goal."[5] Bock offers this formula for resumé writing. Rather than merely listing a job's role, use this formula to explain exactly how what you accomplished benefited the company. You can use it to explain how your goal specifically benefits you overall and your career.

You do all this work because it's best not to make any assumptions about your aspirations. Work it out in writing. For more attainable goals:

- Think about life goals, macro- and micro-goals. Determine **how** and **why** each will get you to where you want to be. Connect a specific rationale to each goal.
- *Focus on pursuing the most critical goals first.*
- Chart out the resources that each goal requires. Check feasibility.
- Schedule relaxing and enjoyable activities to buttress your career goals. Emotional and physical wellness aid achievement. When I asked Fernando Mattei, creative director at BBH New York, what advice he would offer to his 22-year-old self, he said, "Don't stop exercising because of work. You catch up on your career. Sometimes you cannot catch up on your health."

- Be realistic about your expectations for yourself.
- Realize that we often have to sacrifice something or put something else on the back burner to achieve a goal. For instance, if my micro-goal is taking a writing course (after work), that means I will have to sacrifice time with my friends or family to both take the course and complete the assignments. Or I'd have to put another personal project on the back burner, let's say learning a new language.

Remember, despite one's best efforts, stuff happens; *focus on moving forward*, growing, and improving regardless of setbacks.

Make sure to determine what each goal will provide in the short term and long term.

Prune Your List of Goals

Time is valuable. To use it wisely and to accomplish what's most urgent, you have to prioritize your goals. Although each goal is probably a worthy one, it competes with the other for your time and attention!

Once you've set goals, eliminate some. As my wise mother used to say when she thought I was planning too many goals, "You can't dance at two different weddings at the same time." Here's CEO of Berkshire Hathaway Warren Buffet's, legendary three-step method for prioritizing goals, according to Mike Flynn who was Buffet's personal pilot for ten years:

1. Write down your top 25 career goals.
2. Circle your top 5 goals.
3. Move the top 5 to one list and the remaining 20 to a second list. The second list of 20 should get *none* of your attention until you accomplish the first list of 5.[6]

Goals Blueprint Worksheet

For each goal, fill in the blanks.

Resources	
Obstacles	
Time commitment	
What you give up (sacrifices required to achieve a goal)	
What you get	
Timeline	
Work/Life balance	
How the goal contributes to your overall career	
Your thoughts	
Notes	

Figure 4.1 Goals blueprint worksheet

Sticking to Your Plan. Or Not

Regardless of where you are in your career, you should always consider where you want to be, two roles from now (versus just the next one). This way, you can ensure that the next opportunity you're taking is helping you grow in the right direction while staying open to your 5- or 10-year plan changing.

—Zoia Kozakov, product leader at various Fortune 500 companies and start-ups

Due diligence in researching what each career demands will save you time and energy. Talk to people who are in the career fields you desire. Ask a professional or your former professor if the goals you're setting are prudent. Reach out to professionals on LinkedIn to request a few minutes of their time to discuss their careers.

I'm pretty good about achieving my career goals, for the most part. I'm not so good at some personal goals, such as getting enough sleep. So, what I've done that works is congratulate myself when I do go to sleep at a reasonable hour. Surprisingly, giving oneself small affirmations can be a source of motivation.

- Congratulate yourself over even the smallest micro-goal achieved. *Progress principle* is a concept that states the importance of progress in attaining goals. Small successes while working toward a goal contribute to positive emotions, strong motivation, and improved productivity.[7]
- Always replenish your energy with some activity you enjoy.
- Recognize which goals work concurrently with your present job, family commitments, available resources, and life in general.
- Try not to set concurrent goals that will exhaust you.
- Realize that goal fulfillment is a process—it's a journey you're on. Try to appreciate the process. (It's great when my book is published; however, I love the entire process of research and writing even though it's challenging and taxing.) It's about you—who you are; you'll inevitably learn about yourself, which is always interesting. You're learning external things and learning about yourself in the process.
- Become more comfortable with uncertainty; it's part of everyone's life and there's no point in not embracing it. Besides, the more comfortable you become with uncertainty, the better you'll be at creative thinking. (More about creativity in Chapter 8.)
- Find pleasure in the journey or process. It's not always about the end. When I'm designing, I enjoy the design process even if the resulting design isn't what I hoped for or what the client approves.

- Framing your goals with a growth mindset lends itself to greater success. According to Carol S. Dweck, PhD, Lewis and Virginia Eaton Professor of psychology, Stanford University, those who have a growth mindset believe that their abilities can be developed. Since the 2007 publication of Dweck's book, *Mindset: The New Psychology of Success*, a growth mindset has become synonymous with flourishing. Having a growth mindset also puts you in a motivated state of mind. If you think you're growing intellectually and skills-wise, then you'll likely be more motivated.
- It's helpful to stick to your plan. Or not. If a terrific opportunity presents itself, you might have to alter your course of action. Evaluate the benefits of changing course.

How You React to a Fail

There's a witty children's book by Taro Gomi titled, *Everyone Poops*. Well, everyone fails, too. Here's some (not particularly inspirational but definitely) practical advice. I say it's not particularly inspirational because failing stinks. Therefore, we persevere.

Determine what exactly went wrong and right: Imagine that you're one of those storybook regenerating creatures that bounce back to life no matter what. If a goal doesn't work out, figure out why and what went wrong. Not every fail is a complete disaster; there often are good parts of it, for example, you learned something along the way, you enjoyed part of the journey, you met some interesting people, or most importantly, you learned something about yourself.

Reset: You can be more strategic or strategically creative with that information to reset and start again.

Here's a great example of that. Years after his college graduation and work experience in tech companies, Kevin Systrom created a location-based iPhone app—his first tech solo enterprise—called Burbn, which allowed users to check in at particular locations, make plans for future check-ins, earn points for hanging out with friends, and post pictures of their meet-ups. Burbn wasn't a hit, but Systrom kept tweaking the app, paying close attention to how people were using it. He brought on another programmer, Mike

Krieger, and the pair used analytics to determine exactly how their customers were using Burbn. Their findings? People weren't using Burbn's check-in features at all. What they were using were the app's photo-sharing features.[8]

After analyzing their data and realizing people were enthusiastically posting and sharing photos, Systrom and Krieger focused on just that—a photo-sharing app we now know as Instagram.

Acknowledge strengths and weaknesses: When you have a clear understanding of what transpired, you can acknowledge either the strengths and weaknesses of the project or of yourself. For example, when one of my books didn't sell well, I had to acknowledge that I didn't promote it. At all. It wasn't just the publisher who dropped the ball. I acknowledged that failure, and now I know I must promote a book for it to succeed.

It's good to assess whether you need someone's assistance or to sharpen your skills in a particular area before you resume. Did you learn anything about yourself that can help you succeed in the future?

> Embrace your failures, adjust your goals, and KEEP WORKING! Every success is the product of many failures.
> —Gabriel Fuentes, director, Design Action Studio for Research, Architecture, and Urbanism, and assistant professor of Architecture, Kean University

Self-compassion: Blaming yourself gets in the way of moving on. As I said earlier, everyone fails. Students, professionals, athletes, AI experts, creative directors—everyone. Do you think every scientist's experiment works? Has a NASA space shuttle ever failed? Have you seen government legislation fail? Some people hold irrational beliefs about success and failure. It's rational to realize that failure is part of any learning process.

Some failures are preventable. Some are unavoidable given how complex a problem is or with lots of combinations of people and moving parts. Some can provide new knowledge or information.

When you have a positive self-perception, you'll be more inclined to rise and try again or reset and tackle a new endeavor. Tolerance of negative outcomes is best-practice.

Unattainable from the start: Assess the goal and outcomes to see if the goal was within your reach or unattainable from the outset.

Beneficial side effects: Did you learn anything?

> There is a supreme moment of destiny calling on your life. Your job is...to hear that.... And sometimes when you're not listening, you get taken off track. You get in the wrong marriage, the wrong relationship, you take the wrong job, but it's all leading to the same path. There are no wrong paths....There is no such thing as failure really, because failure is just that thing trying to move you in another direction. So you get as much from your losses as you do from your victories, because the losses are there to wake you up.
> —Oprah Winfrey, from Winfrey's lecture to Stanford Graduate School of Business students[9]

Cautions

No matter your goal, it's important to stay motivated. If I were to set a goal, such as getting one more hour of sleep tonight, I'm fairly confident I could achieve that goal. But, if my daughter were to catch a cold or I had a deadline moved up, well, even that easy goal of one more hour of sleep would fail. Achieving even the smallest micro-goals means work and commitment. When you know that things can go awry, develop the ability to reset and forge ahead.

Recognizing your own limits is key, as well as recognizing that there are factors beyond your control that become obstacles or interfere with your best-laid plans. That's why it's important to honestly assess each goal and realize that some goals are draining, challenging, or take a lot of time. While the potential outcomes of other goals are extremely beneficial.

Finding Your Career Path by Mark S. Robinson, brand builder, consultant, and author of *Black on Madison Ave*

Figure 4.2 Mark S. Robinson, brand builder, consultant, and author

Photographer: Tess Steinkolk

Mark Robinson has spent more than forty years in advertising at some of the industry's most prestigious agencies. He has been featured in *Fortune* magazine, the *New York Times*, the *Wall Street Journal*, and *Advertising Age*. Mark is a past member of the American Advertising Federation's Multicultural Marketing Leadership Council, a national touring lecturer for the American Educational Foundation, and an ongoing mentor for MAIP (Minority Advertising Internship Program) for the American Association of Advertising Agencies. Mark lives in Connecticut and is a highly sought-after strategist and advisor to various clients, including political campaigns and community organizations.

Finding your career path will not always be a carefree parade along the yellow brick road, but it probably will have many of the same unexpected twists and turns, challenges and moments of dark uncertainty on your journey. But with the right attitude and perspective, you can make it to the Emerald City.

Most people begin adulthood wholly uncertain of what they want to do with their life, uncertain and overwhelmed with anxiety about what the right path and right choice should be. For many people, that uncertainty lingers and looms like a shadow behind them for many, many years. For some, it can sap the joy from whatever choices and actions they take in life. My own experiences have taught me a few important lessons. Some of those lessons might be worth sharing.

Many of us tend to romanticize our career path. We think that choosing a career is like the search for our one true soulmate, the one who will be with us forever. I think that's a mistake. If you spend a few years at a Wall Street bank or a corporate law firm, and discover that it simply is not what you thought it would be, there are no chains on your ankle. Go find something new. When you started, you had no actual experience to judge by. Now you do. Use that knowledge to make a better choice, a more fulfilling choice. Afraid of being "graded poorly" for making bad choices? That will only happen if you fail to learn and grow from the experience. If you can do that, you're way ahead.

Another way that some of us tend to romanticize our career path is with the classic piece of advice, *"Find a job doing something you love and you will never have to work a day in your life."* What a horrible piece of advice. It's selling you a fantasy that has no basis in reality. And for two reasons. First, (and I apologize if this is harsh) never love a job, because a job will never love you back. It is an expectation that can only lead to heartbreak and disappointment. Instead, love what *you* do. Love yourself doing that thing you do. Find fulfillment (and joy) in the truly unique way that you do the job, the special things that you bring to your work.

Second, that tired old axiom about *"never working a day in your life"* is simply not true. Even at the greatest jobs in the whole world, there are going to be days that are just plain awful. There are going to be days when you go home, have a drink and a good cry. And there are occasionally going to be mornings when you just can't face going to work. Even in the most wonderful jobs. That's just real life. But some people hit those days and think, *"This isn't supposed to happen! I'm supposed to be happy all the time."* Well, you're not. Sometimes, even if you weren't the one to make the situation bad, it will be your job to make the situation better. And sometimes you just have to hunch your shoulders and wait for the rain to stop. It will.

I'm sorry if I make it sound hard. (That is, after all, why they call it "work.") I have been working in advertising and marketing for 44+ years, occasionally trying different things. I can honestly say that my work has done for me all of the things that I have wanted it to do. I haven't always made the best choice, but I learned from my experience and that ultimately put me a step ahead.

Your Career Aspirations and Goals

Let's go back to that unsettling question, "Where do you see yourself in five years?"

Whether you're not sure where you see yourself years from now, or you do know where you want to be, planning for the future focuses your attention toward relevant and productive activities that not only energize you but also move you forward.

Not Sure Which Goals to Pursue

If your career or life goals are still unknown, or you don't know which ones are worthwhile, a good course of action is exploring career paths through research and networking—talking to people in various careers as well as extending your education through continuing education courses.

As a general rule, it's worth pursuing goals that expand your expertise and transferable skills.

Goals Checklist

* Break your goals down into macro- and micro-goals. Start with the macro-goal and determine which micro-goals will aid in achieving the macro-goal.

- Attach a specific rationale to every goal. Understand why you want to achieve each and every goal. What is driving you? Once you fully understand why you want to achieve something, it might be easier to see if that's a good goal to set or if you need to rethink it.
- Be realistic about your expectations. Expect that what you want to achieve might not work out. It's always better to realize that and figure out ways to pivot, find other options, refresh, reset, or rethink. Setbacks happen.
- Focus on growth. Whether you're forging ahead or have a setback, focus on acquiring knowledge and skills rather than a romanticized notion of success. When you grow from any experience, you enrich your career. Uphold your commitment to perseverance.

Your macro-goal can and likely will change over time as you learn more about yourself and what you like or dislike about certain work environments. Revisit the exercises in this book regularly to assess if you're on the right track.

Interview: Dr. Joan Fallon

Figure 4.3 Dr. Joan Fallon, founder and CEO of Curemark

Dr. Joan Fallon, founder and CEO of Curemark, is considered a visionary scientist who has dedicated her life's work to championing the health and well-being of children worldwide. Curemark is a biopharmaceutical company focused on the development of novel therapies to treat serious diseases for which there are limited treatment options. The company's pipeline includes a phase III clinical-stage research program for autism, as well as programs focused on Parkinson's disease, schizophrenia, and addiction. The company's first drug, CM-AT, is targeted to treat autism and is in clinical trials having received Fast Track status from the FDA.

Joan holds over four hundred patents worldwide, has written numerous scholarly articles, and lectured extensively across the globe on pediatric developmental problems. She is a former assistant professor at Yeshiva University in the Department of Natural Sciences and Mathematics. She holds appointments as a senior advisor to the Henry Crown Fellows at The Aspen Institute, as well as a distinguished fellow at the Athena Center for Leadership Studies at Barnard College. She is also a member of the Board of Trustees of Franklin & Marshall College and The Pratt Institute. She currently serves as a board member at the DREAM Charter School in Harlem, the PitCCh In Foundation started by CC and Amber Sabathia, Springboard Enterprises, an internationally known venture catalyst that supports women-led growth companies, and Vote Run Lead, a bipartisan not-for-profit that encourages women on both sides of the aisle to run for elected office.

She served on the ADA Board of Advisors for the building of the new Yankee Stadium and has testified before Congress on the matters of business and patents.

Joan is the recipient of numerous awards including being named one of the top 100 Most Intriguing Entrepreneurs of 2020 by Goldman Sachs and 2017 EY Entrepreneur of The Year NY in Healthcare, and she received the Creative Entrepreneurship Award from The New York Hall of Science in 2018.

Joan published her first book, *Goodbye, Status Quo: Reimagining the Landscape of Innovation*, in January 2022. Now as a respected business leader, doctor, and academic, Joan is driven to share what she has learned and the perspectives that brought her success.

Would you please tell us about your career values? How do you stay true to your values?

Values are very important in whatever you do in life, and when we compromise or suspend them to accomplish something, ultimately, the result does not turn out in our favor. When it comes to career values, you should do something you love, not something you think you should do. You should do something that has meaning even if that meaning is limited in scope. Sometimes it means that you create a new space in which to work.

What led you to found Curemark, your own business?

I had my own medical practice when I made a discovery about children with autism. At the time I was unsure whether the discovery would turn out to be helpful but I needed to find out. I knew that discovery was profound, but whether it could lead to a treatment at the time was unknown.

Now, knowing what we know and being able to create a drug that we believe was helpful to children in the clinical trials we conducted, I'm proud to have founded Curemark.

Along with your role as founder and CEO of Curemark, you fulfill other professional roles. For example, you are a board member and professor. How do you manage to wear so many important hats?

Perspective is really important when looking at your own work. Examining the greater world at large and how others are solving problems outside of your own business or life creates greater empathy and an ability to focus on creating change. There is much to learn outside of your own organization that is key to growth and changes within your organization.

What's the importance of being prepared to pivot or change?

John Wooden, the storied, successful basketball coach at UCLA, said, "Flexibility is the key to stability." While that may seem counterintuitive to some, it is clearly true.

As defined in the *Oxford English Dictionary*, flexibility is:

1. The quality of bending easily without breaking
2. The ability to be easily modified
3. The willingness to change or compromise

Holding a concept or a predetermined pathway too tightly can lead to failure. We found that operating in traditional ways during the pandemic led to failure for some businesses. The businesses that were able to pivot or adapt their standard operating procedures were most successful.

You hold over four hundred patents worldwide. Would you please tell us how you became interested in innovation and patenting your ideas?

My brother is a very successful inventor, and he inspired me greatly; he taught me about the importance of patents in business since it protects your ideas and designs. The nation's founders thought highly enough of patents and intellectual property to make patents and trademarks a part of our Constitution. The first Patent and Copyright Acts were passed by Congress in 1790.

Great ideas solve problems, and protecting those ideas so they can mature for the benefit of others is key when we consider growth and scalability, especially for small businesses. This, in turn, can spur job creation and growth and lead to economic independence and prosperity. One of my focuses for the future is to get more women, people of color, those who are economically disadvantaged, and those who live in rural communities to begin to patent their ideas. Traditionally, these have been the groups who are underrepresented in the patent world. Patents are one of the most egalitarian processes we have in this country, and we need more people to take advantage of this.

Why is diversity, equity, and inclusion critical?

Maya Angelou said, "I believe that every person is born with talent," and I wholeheartedly agree.

Talented individuals with divergent points of view, divergent education, and divergent understanding serve to help solve problems in more creative and efficient ways.

Often, when we seek to hire people, we do not conduct a search for talent, but rather for someone who can fill a job description. If that person fits the bill, we can hire them. However, we need to make a conscious effort to find the most talented people who come from different areas and have different backgrounds. If all we did was hire employees who graduated from the same college or university or were from the same city or state, we would not get diversity of thought in our organization: talent exists in all places and in many forms.

What's one piece of advice you can offer about inspiring and empowering others?

Inspiring and empowering others is my number one value as a leader. The best way to empower people is to make sure they have the tools they need to accomplish shared and personal goals. These tools can take many forms, ranging from making sure that your employees have the right software and equipment, to providing sufficient time off for personal matters and unexpected emergencies.

My concern, especially early on in the Curemark journey, was that people were fed well. They were working long hours every day and sometimes did not get home until late in the evening, so ensuring that everyone had a hot meal at lunch was important to me, and we arranged for that to happen each working day.

You've dedicated your career to the betterment of others. Please tell us about why you put people first.

People are why we do what we do. Our company's tagline is, "It's All About The Kids." As we work toward developing novel treatments to meet unmet medical needs—especially in the pediatric population—putting the needs of patients first is paramount. Leadership is about solving problems and, in doing so, improving the lives of others.

Notes

1   Edwin A. Locke and Gary P. Latham, *A Theory of Goal-Setting and Task Performance*, Englewood Cliffs: Prentice-Hall, 1990:10.
2   Edwin Locke, Karyll Shaw, Lise M. Saari, and Gary Latham, "Goal Setting and Task Performance: 1969–1980," *Psychological Bulletin*, 90(1), 125–152. https://doi.org/10.1037/0033-2909.90.1.125
3   Karen Gilchrist, "Work: Psychologists Share Top Tips On How To Hit Your Career Goals in 2022," CNBC.com, December 30, 2021. https://www.cnbc.com/2021/12/30/career-advice-psychologists-tips-for-meeting-your-work-goals-in-2022.html
4   G.T. Doran, "There's a S.M.A.R.T. Way to Write Management's Goals and Objectives," *Management Review*, 1981; 70, 35–36.
5   Laszlo Bock, "My Personal Formula for a Winning Résumé," LinkedIn.com, September 29, 2014. https://www.linkedin.com/pulse/20140929001534-24454816-my-personal-formula-for-a-better-resume/
6   Jory Mackay, "This Brilliant Strategy Used by Warren Buffett Will Help You Prioritize Your Time," *Inc*.com, November 15, 2017. https://www.inc.com/jory-mackay/warren-buffetts-personal-pilot-reveals-billionaires-brilliant-method-for-prioritizing.html
7   Kelsey Alpaio and Rakshitha Arni Ravishankar, "5 Terms to Know Before Setting a Goal," *HBR*.org, December 28, 2021. https://hbr.org/2021/12/5-terms-to-know-before-setting-a-new-goal
8   Megan Garber, "Instagram Was First Called 'Burbn,'" *The Atlantic*, July 2, 2014. https://www.theatlantic.com/technology/archive/2014/07/instagram-used-to-be-called-brbn/373815/
9   "Oprah Winfrey on Career, Life, and Leadership," Stanford Graduate School of Business, 2014. https://www.youtube.com/watch?v=6DlrqeWrczs&t=27s

MAKE A PLAN

How much time would it take you to accomplish your goals? Is it doable in a month? Year? 3 years? More?

What are the #1, #2, and #3 tasks you must complete to achieve your goals?

Write down 3 potential obstacles that could prevent you from actualizing your goals. What's your plan for overcoming those obstacles?

Notes/Research:

CULTIVATING CULTURAL INTELLIGENCE

DOI: 10.4324/9781003395034-6

Upstanding Workplace Citizenship

When John Prendergast visited my class at Kean University, my students and I were hoping for a visit from actor and human rights activist George Clooney, as well. Prendergast is a human rights, anti-corruption activist, and with George Clooney, the co-founder of The Sentry, an investigative and policy team that follows the dirty money connected to war criminals and transnational war profiteers. Prendergast also is the senior advisor of the Clooney Foundation for Justice. Prendergast and Clooney are good friends and colleagues on an urgent mission for justice.

As soon as Prendergast spoke with us, we were so moved we forgot about Clooney (well, pretty much). He said, "Remember that you're going to have countless chances to be a bystander or an upstander. If enough of us choose to be upstanders, we can change the course of history."

My students knew what it meant to be a *bystander*, or someone who is present but does not take part or action; however, most hadn't heard of the term *upstander*, or someone who sees what happens and intervenes, interrupts, speaks up, or takes some kind of action to stop an injustice.

Whether we are upstanders when we witness someone being bullied online, in person, or we take action to stop corruption, or any other vile act, we also can be upstanding members in our workplace. Some find it challenging to intervene; however, being a staunch advocate of equity and social justice also is what it means to be an upstander.

Diversity, Equity, and Inclusion Is a Shared Responsibility

You might think of most diversity, equity, and inclusion (DEI) initiatives as top-down, where the organization's leaders—the people in charge with the most power—institute equal employment opportunities, hiring and retention practices and goals, develop and adopt the DEI tools necessary for effective change, as well as create an inclusive corporate culture. Top-down directives, programs, efforts, and inclusive leadership are critical; however, each of us must take a proactive role for meaningful change to happen.

DEI initiatives advance social justice, are a moral imperative, and a shared responsibility. When you role model inclusiveness, you positively impact individuals, business, and society.

Putting DEI into the context of early leadership development, decency, respect, and good citizenship are about understanding the importance of individual DEI advocacy. Developing and embracing inclusive traits and behaviors contribute to a healthier society. It might sound Pollyannaish, but it does take all of us working together to achieve equity.

When asked about whether organizational diversity training initiatives work, Robert Livingston, a lecturer at the Harvard Kennedy School, who works as both a bias researcher and a diversity consultant, has a simple proposal: "Focus on actions and behaviors rather than hearts and minds."[1]

Cultivate Your Cultural Intelligence

In order to value the unique perspectives, voices, and contributions of everyone, cultivate your *cultural intelligence*—the capacity to function effectively and respectfully with people from different cultures as well as across different cultures. That capacity involves valuing diversity, being cognizant of your own culture and of possible bias, navigating cultural differences, and actively acquiring knowledge of other cultures and contexts.

Whether you realize it or not, you have a personal worldview, which sounds rather fancy but is a product of any individual's existence. Dr. Alison Gray, a consultant psychiatrist, defines *worldview* as, "a collection of attitudes, values, stories and expectations about the world around us, which inform our every thought and action."[2] Your worldview informs your thinking and behavior; it's based on your values, attributes, your family's and community's values, and shaped by your age, experiences, education, inherited/learned assumptions, and expectations. Your culture, race, ethnicity, gender identity or expression, sexuality, neurocognition, socioeconomic group, friend group, and other factors affect your worldview because they are part and parcel of the background and experiences that have shaped you. Once you recognize the factors that shape and impact your worldview, it's easier to understand that others have different worldviews, experiences, and expectations that are equally valid. Different worldviews are just that—different—not qualitative. There is a caveat, however: intelligent people are adept at engaging in moral reasoning. Their worldviews reject hate, racism, oppression, and supremacy; instead, they embrace a set of ethical principles and avoid morally objectionable thinking.

Your worldview influences your perceptions of the world, political discourse, society, other cultures, and countries. Your worldview affects how you perceive, think, feel, and experience the world and others. According to Holmes et al., "Worldview beliefs are existential, evaluative, or prescriptive beliefs about what exists, what is good, and how people should act."[3] They powerfully affect behavior and can lead to false or faulty assumptions and judgments about others.

You bring your worldview to work with you, which affects how you manage relationships with colleagues, supervisors, and leadership. Learning about your colleagues' cultures improves working relationships and collaborative efforts. "People often are willing to share aspects of their culture when they see that you want to make the relationship work. In turn, they may be more inclined to be sympathetic to your cultural differences as well," says Bhaskar Pant, executive director of MIT Professional Education.[4]

Interestingly, some inclusive traits and creative thinking traits overlap; for example, curiosity about people, cultures, and experiences, as well as courage are traits that creative thinkers and DEI advocates have in common. (More on creativity in Chapter 8.)

Being Proactive

One step beyond being aware of how your worldview colors your thinking is to renounce cultural stereotypes, which negatively influence and distort reasoning and expectations. Valuing cultural differences enables you to build better working relationships with people from different groups, as well as form deeper connections with others. To do this, you have to be cognizant of implicit bias (prejudice that is present but not consciously recognized), which causes people to believe their culture is superior to others, thinking of differences as deficits rather than as informing and invaluable different perspectives. For example, although someone might explicitly state that people with different gender identities should have equal opportunity, someone could have an implicit bias about gender as it relates to specific careers.

Adopting a discovery mindset to seek enlightenment and working to raise your cultural intelligence will aid all aspects of your career; these actions prepare you for a leadership role. Learning about diverse cultures, conventions, and practices, being culturally aware during interactions with colleagues and clients, avoiding assumptions and generalizations, and being inclusive are not only beneficial for your career and organization but also for society. Furthering self-awareness is a lifelong mission.

Be a DEI Champion

Being an advocate or ally starts with treating each individual with dignity and respect. It also entails recognizing discrimination or organizational hegemony. Learning about issues of social justice, such as privilege and systemic oppression, as well as educating yourself about the heritage and cultures of different people, especially people from historically marginalized and underrepresented groups, leads to greater understanding and much improved interpersonal collegial relationships. "You are only as successful as the relationships you build and the people you help," advises Gabriel Fuentes, director of Design Action Studio for Research, Architecture, and Urbanism, and assistant professor of Architecture at Kean University.

As I mentioned before, some people don't realize they carry implicit bias. People also might not realize the effects of denigrative humor or comments, targeting groups based on age, race, ethnicity, sexual orientation, socioeconomic group, physical appearance, religious affiliation, gender identity, gender expression, neurodiversity, veteran status, marriage status, life experiences (e.g., immigration status or health status), or aiming at people living with disabilities, intellectual or physical. Speaking up in a civil manner to say that kind of humor stifles inclusion, adversely affects people, or is unacceptable can help a co-worker understand the implicit harm.

The goal is to raise people up and tear down barriers.

> I would say that my role as a scientist is really about my passion and purpose for the world and for giving back to the world.
> —Dr. Kizzmekia Corbett, assistant professor of Immunology and Infectious Diseases, Harvard University School of Public Health

Collaboration and Teams

Always ask, "Who's *not* on this team?" Being an advocate means raising awareness of who doesn't have a seat at the table or a voice in the discussion. To help my students examine their ideas, I wrote a social justice treatise. Answering the following questions, which are extracted from that treatise, will not only set you on the path to ensuring your thinking or behavior is responsive to diversity, equity, and inclusion but also make your thinking more consequential:

- Have I considered how people of different ethnicities may identify with my ideas or my solution to a work problem?
- Am I employing a stereotype or trope relative to race, ethnicity, gender identity, sexuality, religion, people living with a disability or a neurodiversity, or age?
- Have I tried swapping a group for that of another race, ethnicity, gender, age, sexual orientation, or religion? If so, do any stereotypes emerge?
- Does my idea or solution contribute to any hegemonic systems of oppression?
- Have I thought about elevating equity? Am I advocating for social justice?
- Am I welcoming opportunities to obtain different perspectives and learn about diversity?
- Am I willing to engage in respectful dialogue (and not debate)?

Respectful Workplace Spaces, Conversations, and Discussions

Even if the organization's leaders aren't doing their best to create a safe workplace environment for dialogue where everyone and anyone can express ideas and concerns, you can contribute to creating one through tolerance and mindful listening. We learn as much from each other as from the leadership.

> A diverse mix of voices leads to better discussions, decisions, and outcomes for everyone.
>
> —Sundar Pichai, CEO, Alphabet

Words and terminology matter. Explicit inclusive behavior, such as using inclusive language and being aware of how people identify themselves, helps build awareness, encourages openness (which is critical to collaboration), and combats injustice on a personal level. Becoming skilled at inclusiveness, at connecting with others, aids teamwork, collegiality, and equity.

"Interpersonal Inclusion" by Dr. Juliet Bourke

Figure 5.1 Dr. Juliet Bourke, professor and author

Photographer: Pablo Hernandez

Dr. Juliet Bourke is a professor of Practice in the Business School at the University of New South Wales in Sydney, Australia and sits on a number of boards. Formerly a partner in Human Capital at Deloitte, she continues to advise global organizations on diversity, equity, and inclusion, particularly inclusive leadership and interpersonal inclusion. She is well known for her thought leadership and has published in the *Harvard Business Review* and has spoken at TEDx.

Her most recent book is entitled, *Which Two Heads Are Better Than One?: The extraordinary power of diversity of thinking and inclusive leadership.*

What is interpersonal inclusion?

Interpersonal inclusion refers to the small behaviors exchanged between peers so as to make a team member feel included, i.e., experience a sense of value and connectedness. There are three types of interpersonal inclusion behaviors: instrumental assistance, emotional bond, and embodied connection. *Instrumental assistance* refers to the discretionary help one peer gives to another (e.g., information or contacts) to enable the performance of work tasks. *Emotional bond* refers to the care, support, and personal interest team members demonstrate toward their peers (e.g., by joking, socializing, and venting). *Embodied connection* refers to the ways team members use their corporeal being to create and monitor physical connectivity (e.g., through body language, the sharing of physical space in the office or home backgrounds while on video calls).

Why is interpersonal inclusion important?

The capability to work with peers in a diverse team is of growing importance given the rise of teamwork to solve complex problems and create production efficiencies, flatter hierarchies, and diverse workforces. If you think about it, we each have so many more relationships with peers than we do with leaders. You could think of peer relationships as the sand on a beach, and leaders as big rocks dotted along the beach. Peers literally make the place what it is, but sometimes all we talk about are the rocks.

How does interpersonal inclusion work?

My research on interpersonal inclusion found that from a psychosocial perspective, team members who experience interpersonal inclusion with a peer are more likely to feel motivated and energetic about work, psychologically safe, and comfortable than team members who experience interpersonal exclusion. These behaviors are critical to leveraging and growing human capital. In addition, in a virtuous circle, behaviors of interpersonal inclusion demonstrated by one peer trigger the social exchange of reciprocal behaviors by the recipient peer. Hence, the exchange of instrumental assistance (e.g., verbal endorsement), triggers the exchange of another direct or diffuse positive behavior (e.g., the sharing of information) and this of course benefits both peers. Finally, interpersonal inclusion between peers is a gateway to inclusion between a team member and the larger group, thus opening up access to an even broader set of resources.

Why are insights about interpersonal inclusion empowering?

Research and practice regarding diversity has focused on creating inclusive workplaces via improving organizational processes and policies as well as leadership behaviors. While these foci are important and foundational, individual employees who are not policymakers or leaders can feel a lack of agency in terms of co-creating an inclusive workplace. The identification of interpersonal inclusion as a powerful tool to create a more inclusive and effective workplace empowers individuals to be change agents. Indeed, my research found that half of the research participants deliberately initiated inclusive behaviors with a peer to not only trigger a positive reciprocal exchange of resources, but to generate a sense of personal agency and control over their environment. In other words, feeling included was not a passive experience by which an individual waited for an organizational process/ policy to be enacted, or a leader to behave inclusively towards them, it could also be catalyzed by a team member focusing at the micro- level on their peer relationships. In other words, when a peer included others, it made them feel included as well.

Seek Diverse Perspectives

The need for innovation to grow, compete, and transform has never been greater—and we believe diversity is essential to driving this innovation.
—Julie Sweet, CEO, Accenture North America

Multiple perspective-taking allows you to look at a situation, an idea, a life lived, or an event from the viewpoints of people who are different from you—those who have had different experiences. That shift in perspective adds a fuller dimension to your thinking and problem-solving. As I mentioned earlier, we each have our unique view of the world shaped by our experiences, communities, families, and education—the lens through which we see the world and ourselves in it. Gillian Ku, professor of Organizational Behavior and chair of the Organizational Behavior Faculty at London Business School, defines *perspective-taking* as, "the active cognitive process of imagining the world from another's vantage point."[5]

Perspective-Taking

Taking multiple perspectives—that is, looking at a goal, a business or subject-based problem, a partially realized idea, or a full-fledged idea from viewpoints different from your own—helps you perceive multiple scenarios, views, and benefits, ultimately resulting in smarter decisions and better ideas that appeal in more meaningful ways to more people and more engaged stakeholders.

Embrace diversity through inclusive conversations; this can be done during ideation, a problem-solving phase, or problem-finding, a process of identifying problems worth solving at the outset. Problem-finding can be seeking out problems that need to be solved that are being neglected, or that no one else has noticed. In an experiment, the researchers' results "point to perspective taking as an important mechanism to unlock diversity's potential for team creativity."[6] Learning about the experiences of others and gaining knowledge from others allow you to consider elements and viewpoints you didn't think to consider before, which will help you connect, learn, and perform better.

Can you think of a work situation where obtaining the perspectives of others would have been advantageous? How might perspective-taking improve the short- and long-term outcomes of work issues, problems, and solutions?

Fresh perspectives also lead to additional questions, which is crucial to solving a problem well or recognizing an issue you had not known existed. By asking more questions of diverse people, you keep widening your scope and the impact of your idea. Here are four questions to ask:

- What goal can I set to have the best possible outcomes for the most possible people?
- Is there an issue I hadn't considered before I took multiple perspectives?
- Is there a benefit that is more equitable?
- Is there a question someone else raised that moves my thinking forward?

Inclusive and diverse teams are not only more equitable but also combat *groupthink*—a mode of thinking that occurs when individuals of a highly cohesive, insular group or an in-group strive for consensus and might avoid or override alternate viewpoints, ideas, actions, or dissent. Also, an in-group might be unfamiliar with outside perspectives, unwilling or reluctant to engage with external experts and to explore or engage in debate.

> When it comes to diversity in a workplace, it isn't just about the individuals we hire with varied backgrounds, but also the MacGyvers in our organizations who bring those individuals together to make something no one expected, a brain trust that thinks differently and celebrating one's culture applied in a different context.
>
> At MRM we are always looking for different minds and the MacGyvers who bring them together.
>
> —Harsh Kapadia, EVP, chief creative officer at MRM New York

If you view a problem you have to solve or an issue from other perspectives, you will begin to see how age, gender identity or expression, neurodivergence, culture, race, ethnicity, religious affiliation, socioeconomics, health status, or community characteristics might affect and ultimately amplify your thinking or solution. In a conversation with Harsh Kapadia, chief creative officer at MRM New York, a leading marketing agency, he told me that not only will you get unfamiliar perspectives from a diverse group, but you likely will get *different problem-solving* input as well. When you augment your thinking through inclusion, you have a greater pool of viewpoints and you will find valuable insights into other people that will lead you to more *significant* ideas and solutions.

Of course, obtaining multiple perspectives means listening intently. Whether you're leading or following, no matter the situation, attentive listening is critical to understanding what other people think or feel. When obtaining multiple perspectives and listening to other people's experiences, it is also extremely important not to question the validity of what anyone is saying because it's not in your realm of experience or cultural knowledge. This shuts down open dialogue. Just as in brainstorming, the loudest or most persistent voice can drown out other worthwhile statements or ideas. If you belong to an underrepresented group, accepting allyship is important as well.

As a citizen and an early leader, consciously elect to build inclusion.

"Be the Voice for Diversity" by Mark S. Robinson, brand builder, consultant, and author of *Black on Madison Avenue*

It isn't hard to think of examples of ads we have seen—whether print or digital or broadcast—that were unabashed embarrassments, ads that caused brands to lose loyal customers, goodwill and market share. We see those ads and we say, "That never would have happened if there had been a person of color in the room." (Or perhaps a person from the LGBTQ+ community.) Chances are, it was the absence of those faces and voices, the absence of authentic diverse experiences that contributed to the failure of the advertising.

It is, however, time we accepted our shared responsibility for that failure. It's time we acknowledged that unless we are speaking up and speaking out, we too are enablers of the status quo. We are the ones helping to keep things just the way they are, which is not good enough. Too many of us feel it is not our job to tell our bosses or the HR department that they need to do a better job of recruiting, interviewing and hiring diverse talent. But, if it's not our job, then who? There is no justification for being a bystander to the absence of diversity. Whenever there is a crowd of bystanders, everyone assumes that someone else will step up. No one does. It needs to be you. It needs to be each of us.

And, as in all things, do not simply complain. Bring ideas, recommendations. Referrals if you can. You might be a thorn in someone's side, but you might be the agency's champion, their game-changer.

If you are the voice of difference in the strategic and creative development process, for heaven's sake, make sure your voice is heard. You weren't hired to be a wallflower or a yes-person. You were hired to make a difference. Encourage, support and build upon the good ideas of others. Explain why some ideas really aren't that good, and how—together—you can make them better.

Equity

Capuchin monkeys prefer grapes to cucumbers. What would happen if a person were to give cucumbers to one capuchin monkey who could see the same person give grapes to their neighboring capuchin monkey?

Dr. Sarah Brosnan is a distinguished professor in the Departments of Psychology and Philosophy and the Neuroscience Institute at

Georgia State University, where she also directs the Comparative Economics and Behavioral Sciences Lab. One of Dr. Brosnan's most famous studies (approximately twenty years ago) "looked at how monkeys responded when given an inferior treat when compared to their partner." If you haven't seen it, I urge you to watch her TED Talk on why monkeys and humans are wired for fairness, which has been viewed nearly 1.5 million times, and to read about it in an interview with Brosnan in APA.org. In short and very generally, one goal was to see how animals react to unfairness; there were several control groups. The research team took two monkeys from the same social group. The monkeys' task was to trade a token; when they did that, the monkeys received a food reward. When the researcher gave cucumbers to both monkeys, the monkeys accepted and ate the cucumbers. But in one control group, "when their partner got a grape, they were much more likely to refuse their cucumber, which suggests that they aren't as enthusiastic about those cucumbers when their partner is getting something better."[7] What happens when unfairness strikes—when one monkey gets a grape and the other gets a cucumber in exchange for the same tokens? The monkey that did not get the grape hurled the cucumber back at the handler.

Why bring up cucumbers and grapes?

According to Dr. Brosnan, "Pay one monkey with a delicious grape and another with a ho-hum cucumber for the same amount of work, the monkey that got the lesser reward will probably quit working for you. The monkey may even throw the vegetable back at you, even though monkeys are usually happy to receive cucumbers."[8]

In the workplace, many individuals' perceptions of fairness relate to their day-to-day experiences, which inevitably impacts the organization.

Perception of fairness improves employee performance by up to 26 percent and retention by up to 27 percent. According to Gartner research, to create a higher-fairness experience for all employees, organizations need to ask themselves four key questions: (1) Do employees have the information they need to succeed at their jobs and advance their careers?, (2) Do they feel supported?, (3)

Does everyone get a fair chance at internal opportunities?, and (4) Do leaders and managers recognize employee contributions?[9]

In the workplace, people want organizational justice. They also want to be treated fairly in interpersonal relationships with colleagues. The corporate culture must have an assurance of psychological safety. It is up to each individual to treat colleagues with the same amount of respect and value. Organizations need to ask themselves those questions; however, treating people fairly based on who they are as unique individuals rather than on being a member of specific groups creates a tolerant diversity climate, though acceptance is also a key factor. According to Hofhuis et al., "Diversity climate, defined as an organizational climate characterized by openness towards and appreciation of individual differences, has been shown to enhance outcomes in culturally diverse teams."[10]

DEI and Early Leadership

Wise leaders create conditions that allow every member to flourish. In Chapter 1, I wrote about values. When you adopt DEI as a core value, you commit to a more just society. Below is a shorthand guide to committing to DEI and empowering all.

Guide to Elements of Inclusive Leadership

Fairness: Treat people fairly. Though each of us belongs to a community or hails from a culture, treat people based on their distinct individuality rather than on assumptions or notions about a group.

Respect: Value each individual's talent, work, input, and contributions, what each member of an organization brings to the table. Speak to and treat each individual with civility and the regard due to any sentient being. Often, respecting the ideas of others entails humility or deference.

Respectful Curiosity: Ask people questions. Perspective-taking should be ongoing. Don't assume; assumptions are dangerous. Obtaining divergent perspectives is an opportunity to expand your comprehension of a wider realm.

Leverage: Divergent perspectives lead to insights, knowledge, and understanding others' experiences and points of view. In an organizational setting, leverage those insights and identity-related knowledge to build better. Learning to manage across differences can lead to creative solutions.

Optimum Collaboration: DEI means a greater talent pool; everyone deserves opportunities. A survey by the Boston Consulting Group found that "breakthrough innovators" cast a wider net for ideas.[11]

Organization's Mission: If an organization articulates and disseminates an inclusivity and diversity mission, where equity is key, then it's easier for everyone to get behind it.

Reflect on how you advance DEI in your professional life. Contributing to the construction of an inclusive corporate culture and valuing the unique perspectives and contributions of everyone build a better workplace for everyone.

Commit to ensuring workplace diversity, equity, and inclusion. Actions to work by:

- Get multiple perspectives. Oppose groupthink.
- Advocate for diverse teams. Address systemic exclusion.
- Do not force assimilation to the dominant culture.
- Be inclusive. Fight exclusion and cliques.
- Use broad evaluation criteria to honor diversity of thinking and ways.
- Practice mindful listening. Resist shutting people down.
- Value each person as a unique individual. Don't denigrate or dehumanize anyone.
- Respect people living with disabilities, both physical and intellectual. Respect everyone's race, ethnicity, gender identity and expression, religion, sexuality, age, neurodiversity, and socioeconomic group.
- Add what you think is an imperative:_____
_____.

Interview: Dr. Arti Agrawal

Figure 5.2 Dr. Arti Agrawal, adjunct associate professor at the University of Technology Sydney, and CEO and founder of Vividhata Pty Ltd

Photographer: John Stevenson/Optica

Arti's current professional positions reflect her dual passions: science and social justice.

She is an adjunct associate professor in the School of Electrical and Data Engineering at the University of Technology Sydney (UTS). She is also the CEO and founder of a Vividhata Pty Ltd, a diversity and inclusion consulting company.

"Vividhata" means diversity in Sanskrit. The company epitomizes Arti's vision to globally advance and mainstream diversity and inclusion initiatives in all sectors of society. In setting up Vividhata, Arti is guided by her lived intersectional experiences of being a female immigrant from India, diversity leader and coach, person of color, physicist, and proud member of the global LGBTQIA+ community.

Arti's work experience history reflects her passions: she was director of Inclusion, Diversity and Involvement at Anthony Nolan Trust, a blood cancer charity; and before that she was director of Women in Engineering at UTS, along with holding a substantive Associate Professorship in Electrical Engineering. Previously, Arti worked at City, University of London from 2005 to 2017 in the Department of Electrical Engineering. She has been a Royal Society postdoctoral fellow, and her PhD was on modeling methods for optical components, completed at the Indian Institute of Technology Delhi in 2005.

Arti's research interests lie in optics: modeling of photonic components such as solar cells, optical fibers, sensors, lasers, etc. She is an expert on numerical methods for optics such as Finite Element Method (FEM). She has written a book on FEM and edited a book on trends in computational photonics.

Arti leverages her technical expertise in data and numerical analysis along with lived experience and work in diversity and inclusion to DEI for complex organizations. She has worked on inclusion and equity on projects for international tech bodies, universities, charities and schools. She takes an intersectional view of identity in her approach to DEI.

Arti is a senior member of the IEEE and Optica. She was awarded the 2020 IEEE Photonics Society Distinguished Service Award for exceptional contributions to the Photonics Society as a champion of diversity and inclusion initiatives. She was also awarded the OSA Diversity and Advocacy Recognition in 2020 for an unwavering dedication to promoting diversity and inclusion throughout the global optics and photonics community.

How can someone exert influence in their workplace?

In a global world, we work, play, and live with people different from us in many ways. People want to see their identity reflected in the services and products they use. They want fair treatment at work in a positive culture. Thus, celebrating diversity by being inclusive of differences is critical to success for both individuals and organizations. Moreover, a fair and just society requires DEI built into all our systems in line with the U.N.'s 17 Sustainable Development Goals.

Young professionals can influence their environment at work, study, and in their communities. Being vocal about DEI, engaging and leading DEI initiatives, and articulating both the social and business benefits are some approaches to promote DEI.

Any advice for women in STEM?

Following one's passion and being true to one's values can help navigate moments of confusion in STEM careers. Let your passion be your guiding star. Create a strong network (including women) at work; this will help you weather difficult times when there is pressure. It will reduce the sense of isolation many women face. Go out of your way to find women at work. Support other women!

You benefit from the struggles of countless women before you, which has resulted in better conditions for you: the vote, right to work, own property, etc. Ask yourself what will you contribute to this ongoing struggle for women's equality? What will be your legacy? Ensure you have a fulfilling life outside of work too, to have positive energy from fun and learning other skills that balance your personality.

Why is having a mentor or sponsor important?

Mentors can help in innumerable ways that depend on what one wants. I have had mentoring to create a strategy for my larger career goals, in navigating the culture and politics of my organization, and for smaller goals such as developing skills in a particular area, applying for a promotion, etc.

Sponsors can help open doors that you can't open on your own. They use their influence to help you progress and make opportunities available for the next step. There can be some overlap between sponsorship and mentorship, but they are distinct.

What's the importance of being prepared to pivot or change?

Change is inevitable. Making change work for you is better than change being forced upon you by trauma. Inertia and fear of the unknown often keep us rooted to situations, at times, unfavorable ones. Being able to pivot and make change a positive part of life is important. It allows us to design our lives for our changing needs, and to create the opportunities we desire.

Any advice on setting macro- and micro-career goals?

Micro-goals are great for keeping momentum and progress without being overwhelmed when faced with larger-than-life goals. Macro-goals are the bigger picture that drive us—the dreams we want to fulfill. The pursuit of these and the learning they bring is more important than success/failure.

How do you stay true to your values?

Occasionally when I lose sight of my values, I feel a lot of emotional dissonance and distress. That pain serves as a prod, guiding me by my values compass. For that reason, I articulate my values on paper when I feel change creeping up. I align my macro- and micro-goals to these values. To retain sight of my values, I remind myself why I do what I do almost daily.

How did you form your career interests?

As a child I was fascinated by stars. Watching Carl Sagan's show, *Cosmos*, crystallized this interest into a lifelong love of science and was the basis of choosing science as a career.

Notes

1 Jesse Singal, "What If Diversity Trainings Are Doing More Harm Than Good?" *New York Times*, January 17, 2023. https://www. nytimes.com/2023/01/17/opinion/dei-trainings-effective. html?searchResultPosition=1

2 Alison J. Gray, "Worldviews," *International Psychiatry*, August 1, 2011; 8(3): 58–60. https://www.ncbi.nlm.nih.gov/pmc/articles/ PMC6735033/

3 Oliver S. Holmes, Bruce M. Findlay and Roger Cook, "Worldview Psychology and the Representation of Spirituality, Naturalism, and Agnosticism: Conceptualization and Psychometric Measurement," *Australian Journal of Psychology*, April 13, 2021; 73(4), 535–547. https://doi.org/10.1080/00049530.2021.1918534,   https://www.tandfonline.com/doi/full/10.1080/00049530.2021.1918534

4 Bhaskar Pant, "Different Cultures See Deadlines Differently," *HBR*.org, May 23, 2016. https://hbr.org/2016/05/different-cultures-see-deadlines-differently

5 Gillian Ku and Kathy Brewis, "The Power of Perspective-Taking," London Business School, February 1, 2017. https://www.london.edu/think/power-of-perspective-taking

6 I. J. Hoever, D. van Knippenberg, W. P. van Ginkel, and H. G. Barkema, "Fostering Team Creativity: Perspective Taking as Key to Unlocking Diversity's Potential," *Journal of Applied Psychology*, July 2012; 97(5), 982–996. https://doi.org/10.1037/a0029159

7 Kim Mills, "Speaking of Psychology," APA.org. https://www.apa.org/news/podcasts/speaking-of-psychology/fairness

8 Sadie F. Dingfelder, "Nice by Nature?" American Psychological Association, *Monitor*, September 2009; 40(8), 58. https://www.apa.org/monitor/2009/09/moral-behavior

9 Brian Kropp, Jessica Knight, and Jonah Shepp, "How Fair Is Your Workplace?" *HBR*.org, July 14, 2022. https://hbr.org/2022/07/how-fair-is-your-workplace

10 Joep Hofhuis, Pernill Rijt, and Martijn Vlug. "Diversity climate enhances work outcomes through trust and openness in workgroup communication," *SpringerPlus*, 2016: 5. 1-14. https://doi.org/10.1186/s40064-016-2499-4

11 Boston Consulting Group, "The Most Innovative Companies 2014: Breaking Through is Hard To Do," 2014; 6. https://www.bcgperspectives.com/most_innovative_companies

ENSURING SUCCESS: MENTORS & SPONSORS

06

DOI: 10.4324/9781003395034-7

Career-Making Relationships

When I was in graduate school, I had a teaching fellowship, which contributed toward tuition and was the catalyst for my love of teaching. During my second year, a different faculty member headed the graduate program. To put it bluntly, she did not like me. At all. She harassed me. But worst of all, she unilaterally took away my fellowship. Other senior faculty came to my defense, which is when I learned how important it is to have someone who supports you. This also was my first major lesson that fairness and merit do not trump all. At times, it doesn't matter how good you are at what you do or how equitable things are supposed to be, people do not necessarily treat others fairly based on merit.

That's a good-enough reason to heed the following advice that will significantly contribute to the success of your career.

Two career-making professional relationships are mentorship and sponsorship. Mentorship is where someone who is more experienced provides advice, guidance, and feedback. A mentor does not necessarily have to be someone in your workplace; that person can be someone you met at a professional organization or through networking, within or outside your profession. A professor also can serve as a mentor. A sponsor is someone who uses their prestige and position to advocate for you in order to advance your career.

Many people entering the workforce have heard about the importance of mentorship; however, sponsorship is just as important, perhaps even more important if you want to advance. "Mentors provide advice, feedback and coaching through formal or informal relationships, while sponsors use their influence or leadership status to advocate for your advancement or provide you with access to opportunities," explains Julie S. Nugent, senior vice president of Learning & Advisory Services at Catalyst.[1]

"Sponsors differ from mentors in that they advocate for the sponsee, make social connections, and use their own social capital on behalf of the sponsee...Sponsors are advocates and investors. Their support is public and they use their reputation to support yours," advises Marissa King, professor in the School of Management at Yale University, and author of *Social Chemistry: Decoding the Patterns of Human Connection.*[2]

Mentor/Protégé Relationships

During your university years, first internship, or job, finding a mentor helps tremendously. A mentor provides formal or informal coaching, advice, and feedback, whether at your organization or externally. Building an authentic relationship with someone who has something to teach you will help you grow faster than doing it alone.

Seasoned professionals know more and have more experience. Let them share it with you. And, please, for the love of ice cream, don't ignore seasoned professionals' advice the way you might ignore advice from your family. Caveat: Some professionals will offer conflicting advice. Always get more opinions to weigh what's right for you.

Mentors

Mentors help you craft your plan "with ongoing advice, including guidance around career decisions and challenges."[3]

There are two basic types of mentoring:

- *One-on-one mentoring* (in-person or virtual): Mentor and mentee are paired via an organization's program, networking, or some kind of fortunate connection, for example, family, professor, or friend. If part of a formal program, the structure and time frame are established by the program. If not, it's up to the partners to establish them.
- *Group mentoring*: One mentor is matched with a cohort of mentees through a formal program structure that often sets the time frame and undertakings.

The benefits of mentoring include having a reliable confidant who is willing to discuss your plans, learning how to approach work and work-related issues, acquiring general professional development skills, and learning about professional development and networking opportunities.

Some people have the resources to hire a career coach, a paid partner who can help you maximize your professional or personal potential. When hiring a coach, people often have a specific performance-driven outcome in mind, whereas a mentorship is more development driven.[4]

You will get the most out of a mentoring partnership when you set macro- and micro-goals (also called objectives) and determine which skills you want to learn. Be sure to share your goals with your mentor.

Proactively ask for feedback, be discrete, be respectful of the mentor's time and their confidences, and make a commitment to the partnership to take full advantage of the opportunity. Committing to learning from a mentor sets you up for lifelong learning. As in all situations, a positive attitude truly helps.

> Success isn't about the end result, it's about what you learn along the way.
>
> —Vera Wang, designer

Finding a Mentor

It's logical to assume that a good mentor is someone who works in your organization, and who is familiar with your industry, role, and future path there. However, a mentor can come from outside your organization, a professional organization, or a related field.

LinkedIn is a good place to search for and reach out to external professionals. Professional organizations in your city are great resources, too. Some retired professionals are willing to mentor.

Ask for a ten-minute online "coffee meeting" with someone who has experience, which could turn into a real connection. Meet the potential mentor to assess whether this person is a good fit for you. If you respect this person's credentials, but their personality is abrasive, perhaps it's not a good fit. The point is to find someone who will provide sagacious advice about your goals and will be respectful of your personhood. Find a mentor who is willing to have career conversations with you, spend time with you.

Mentorship can be two-way. Perhaps you have knowledge or skills that interest your mentor. An early-career professional can mentor a seasoned colleague, which is beneficial for both people.

Sponsorships

You've likely heard the adage, "It's who you know that counts." That certainly applies to networking and finding a job. Well, in terms of advancement in the workplace, think of it as, "It's who knows you that counts." Put very simply, an acknowledged or respected leader who has taken notice of your good work can open doors.

Think of a time when a close friend or family member had your back or helped you get what you wanted; that kind of support happens in the workplace, too. A sponsor is an influential professional with power who champions you, makes advantageous introductions and connections for you, puts you in the running, and aids your advancement. "Career success is as much a game of getting a sponsor as it is one of performing well," says King.[5]

I recommend watching Carla Harris's TED Talk titled, "How to find the person who can help you get ahead at work." Harris advises,

> You are not going to ascend in any organization without a sponsor. It is the critical relationship in your career. There's not one evaluative process I can think of, whether it's academia, health care, financial services, not one that does not have a human element. There is a measure of subjectivity in who is presenting your case, in what they say, and how they interpret any objective data that you might have…make sure…that sponsor has your best interests at heart, and has the power to get it, whatever it is for you, to get it done behind closed doors.
> —Carla Harris, senior client advisor, Morgan Stanley[6]

Finding a Sponsor

Since most organizations do not appoint sponsors or have sponsorship programs, how do you find a sponsor?

Earn It

Make yourself indispensable.

When it comes to your direct supervisor, make that person's job easier. Be the most reliable person on the team; make sure that person can depend on you to come through 100 percent of the time. Go above and beyond. Align your skills with your team's needs. Make sure you're the person with the critical knowledge, expertise, or unique skills, especially if it's something new that others haven't learned yet.

Make some part of the organization dependent upon your skill set. Of course, many people are replaceable, but the idea is to make your organization feel that they *would not want to* replace you because you're so dependable and efficient, and good at what you do, which leads to being considered an expert.

Everyone you work with or for is a reference.

...Often, someone looking to hire simply asks trusted people if they know of a good candidate. When those opportunities arise, you want your name to be at the top of their mind—as someone smart, collegial and hard working. This is why you must give your all in every job you have, no matter how small... And you must treat everyone around you with respect. Because anyone who knows you could give you a reference, without you being the wiser.
   —Charles Blow, the *New York Times* opinion
   columnist, television commentator, and author[7]

Be a True Expert

Most likely you won't be hired unless you have the requisite skills or expertise. Being an expert on the job means more people seek you out for your knowledge and unique capabilities. People senior to you, perhaps someone who would sponsor you, want you on their team because of how you're viewed—as an expert. This will lead to becoming known throughout the organization.

Volunteer

When my students obtain entry-level positions in advertising agencies and branding companies, I tell them to make themselves indispensable and available, not only to their immediate supervisors or creative directors but also to other more senior colleagues. I encourage them to proactively approach senior colleagues, inquire if they require any support, and offer to lighten their workload by taking on tasks.

You can volunteer to take on stretch projects (assignments that stretch your capabilities), as well.

Find Like-Minded Influential People

You've likely heard that career-making relationships happen on the golf course. That is true. However, other interests and causes, such as being a DEI advocate, serving a nonprofit, or having other avocations can connect you to like-minded people with power. For example, working for a cause or volunteering for a nonprofit organization often unites people who share values and believe in working toward a common goal external to their profession.

Mentorship Evolving into Sponsorship

If your mentor is influential enough to advance your career, that mentor/protégé relationship could develop into a sponsorship.

"To succeed at work, you need someone to advocate for you, to put your name in the hat for stretch assignments, and make introductions," advises King.[8]

Sponsorship Meetings

Some people find in-person meetings more conducive to developing a relationship. Others might prefer remote meetings for convenience, geographic logistics, or scheduling issues. Either way, it's important to make the most of your sponsorship meetings.

- Make the most of your sponsor's time. Do not be late when meeting with them or waste their time or support.
- Cultivate the relationship, even if it's a remote one.
- Create an agenda before the one-on-one meeting.
- Ask key, thought-provoking questions.
- Take *constructive* criticism well and put it in perspective and context. Responding with defensiveness or hostility will not serve your interests in any way.
- Commit to being present and earning your sponsor's trust.

> You want to have humility, but you can't be shy to make clear to your supervisors, your leaders, whomever, what your aspiration is. Otherwise, people are going to just guess. Nobody, I promise you, cares more about your career than you do.
> —Beth Ford, CEO of Land O'Lakes[9]

Differentiate Yourself

Two of the best ways to distinguish yourself are to perform at your personal best no matter the situation, and to graciously take critical feedback from senior colleagues, assessing it for your own betterment. Further ways to differentiate yourself include:

- Positively contribute to the organization.
- Be the go-to person for a specific expertise.
- Attract notice by how well you perform.
- Be inclusive and respectful of others.
- Bring a rational perspective to discussions and collaborative efforts.
- Become known for generating creative or imaginative ideas.

> Most entrepreneurial ideas will sound crazy, stupid and uneconomic, and then they'll turn out to be right.
> —Reed Hastings, co-founder and chairman of Netflix

Interview: Sonya Renee Taylor

Sonya Renee Taylor is a *New York Times* best-selling author, world-renowned activist and thought leader on racial justice, body liberation and transformational change, international award-winning artist, and founder of The Body Is Not an Apology (TBINAA), a global digital media and education company exploring the intersections of identity, healing, and social justice through the framework of radical self-love.

Figure 6.1 Sonya Renee Taylor, author, activist, artist, and founder of the TBINAA company

How did you know you wanted to pursue a career in activism?

I knew that I wanted to do things that had a positive impact on people's lives. The beginning parts of that were social service sector work and nonprofit work. Most of the places where I worked, I was always aware that an individual's circumstances were not just about their individual experiences or behaviors, but they were also part of larger social and political ideas and trends. So, it always made sense to me that any kind of sustainable solutions would have to be across social, political, economic, and personal fronts in order to actually make change. I think I knew that as a kid. I was that kid who said, "We have to stop using Styrofoam at the cookout." And that just continued to evolve.

How have you established yourself as a thought leader?

I don't think I've established myself as a thought leader. I am a person who is vocal; I share my ideas out loud. I enjoy ideating in public. I think I'm a thought leader in so much as I share my ideas out loud, and people are like, "I think I agree with that."

As people have found resonance, they've asked me to say more things, or share my opinions about other subject matter. I have thoughts and people seem to resonate with those thoughts. I suppose that's how you become a thought leader.

How did you realize authoring books would be important to your career?

I started off as a writer; I've been a writer since childhood. Spoken and written words are my favorite mediums; they are the places where I feel compassionate connections. I was a 10-year-old who stated, "I am going to be an author." There was always a part of me that knew that. But the opportunity to actually turn the work I was doing into books always came externally. I was thinking out loud and sharing ideas out loud and publishers asked, "Would you be interested in writing a book about that?" I thought, that's probably the easiest way I'm ever going to get a book deal...so, sure. I think I'm the kind of person who holds a clear vision, a vision about what I want to see in the world, a long-term goal of an endeavor that I'm pursuing. Then if I hold fast to the long-term endeavor that I'm pursuing, life just seems to arrange the smaller steps to get there. That's been a pretty consistent reality for me.

For over a decade, you built an award-winning international performance poetry and poetry slam career. How did this iteration of your journey allow you to find your greater purpose?

My performance poetry career was a phase of my life where I was learning how to make sense of the world through language. It was a period of epiphany—*Oh I see these experiences and I think they have a larger meaning for me, a deeper meaning for me.* Consequently, I've always been the person who thinks that if it has a deeper meaning for me, it must have a deeper meaning for someone else because I can't be the only one. As much as I'd like to think I'm the only one, I recognize that I'm not that special.

Performance poetry was my way to make sense of the world, to experience synthesis through art. I can turn this difficult thing, complicated thing, this tragic thing into something beautiful and something that makes sense to me and something that resonates with someone else's journey. I think it created a foundation of understanding of how to tell a story. I feel like my later work has been, "How do we tell a story about our own identities, about our own bodies that's an empowering one?" One that is a story of triumph, of power, of connection. I think I honed those storytelling skills in the performance poetry world.

What do you wish you had known at the start of your professional journey?

I wish I would have recognized that there's very little in my control and that's actually OK. I spent a lot of years trying to control how things happen, how people perceived me, how I was perceived in this place. I spent a lot of energy trying to control external circumstances rather than relinquish a lot of that control, and lean a bit more into trust. Lean a bit more into it—it's all just a ride beyond the ride. If you grip the rails and close your eyes the whole time, you don't get the fun of the roller coaster.

Please tell us about "radical permission."

The Institute of Radical Permission is a learning space co-created by myself and collaborator, comrade, and friend, adrienne maree brown. adrienne is the author of *Pleasure Activism* and *Holding Change*. We always kept finding each other; there's a connection between pleasure and radical self-love, and allowing life to lead us in an organic way that resembles the natural order of other living things. We found connection in our work; and we found connection in the ways we live and move in life. There's a way that we are tapped into our own freedom and a really expansive experience of possibilities. We don't think of it as happenstance. There was something about the way we were moving that felt similar. We began to collaborate so that we could distill these ideas and share them with other people.

The first thing we did was a live event back in 2020: ideating in real time in front of a 3,000-person audience. We were asking the question, "What would we make together if we made a thing together?" From that sprouted the seeds of the Institute of Radical Permission. We want to talk about how we live these really expansive, liberated lives. We want to talk about our growth edges and learning curves, and where those things show up. And, how we move through our own challenges, fears, and disappointments, so that we can continue being in these liberatory expansive mindsets.

From that we began working together over the course of a year and a half. We looked at elements such as Curiosity, Surrender, Grace, and Satisfaction as the four essential elements of the recipes of our lives, and our own permission for living. Then we built out this institute, this 12-module learning modality that really is about how do we tap into our own inner knowing, and disconnect from our programming and indoctrinations, so that we listen to what is true for us, so that what we're giving ourselves permission to be the most authentic, most aligned, most honest version of ourselves as opposed to being governed by scarcity, governed by systems that demand a certain kind of performance of our humanity in exchange for our needs to be met. Our entire premise is what if none of that is true, and what if life is just waiting for you to give yourself permission to unlock the most authentic parts of yourself.

We've had an amazing time building it and watching people transform into more empowered individuals as a result.

You've wisely advised people that "the body is not an apology." What is the best advice anyone has given to you?

People give me amazing advice all the time. I'm very grateful for it. I'm going to share two pieces that resonate with me.

One is from one of my best friends, Maureen Benson, who always says, "You're not late." That advice changes the way that I move through life. "You're not late" gives me permission to take my time, to not feel as if I'm on some ever-expiring clock, and I'm about to run out; so now I need to rush and I need to make that decision now. It's like nothing actually needs to happen right now.

"You're not late" is one of the best pieces of advice; it ties in so perfectly with my therapist who always says, "There's nothing else but this moment. Can you come back to this moment?" Every time I come back to this moment, this moment is just fine. The thing that I'm worrying about is in another place that is not this moment. It allows me to just take life in these really intentional bitesize morsels that are far more delicious when I'm enjoying them in the moment than when I'm off to the next thing that actually hasn't happened yet. It's taken a lot of practice.

Notes

1 "News & Stories: The Importance of Mentors and Sponsors in Career Development," JPMorgan Chase & Co.com. https://www.jpmorganchase.com/news-stories/the-importance-of-mentors-and-sponsors-in-career-development
2 Marissa King, *Social Chemistry: Decoding the Patterns of Human Connection*, New York: Dutton, 2021: 271.
3 David Nour, "Ascend: The Best Mentorships Help Both People Grow," *HBR*.org, January 5, 2022. https://hbr.org/2022/01/the-best-mentorships-help-both-people-grow

4 Christine Zust, "The Center for Corporate and Professional Development: Know the Difference Between Coaching and Mentoring," Kentstate.edu, https://www.kent.edu/yourtrainingpartner/know-difference-between-coaching-and-mentoring

5 Marissa King, *Social Chemistry: Decoding the Patterns of Human Connection*, New York: Dutton, 2021: 271.

6 Carla Harris, "How to Find the Person Who Can Help You Get Ahead At Work | Carla Harris," *TED*.com, December 13, 2018. https://www.ted.com/talks/carla_harris_how_to_find_the_person_who_can_help_you_get_ahead_at_work?language=en

7 Charles M. Blow, "My Times: Career Advice From a Career in the Trenches," *New York Times*.com, June 5, 2022. https://www.nytimes.com/2022/06/05/opinion/advice-journalism-career.html

8 Marissa King, *Social Chemistry: Decoding the Elements of Human Connection*, New York: Dutton, 2021: 267.

9 Kelsey Doyle, "Beth Ford on Being the Champion of Your Own Career," Graduate School of Stanford Business.edu, July 7, 2021. https://www.gsb.stanford.edu/insights/beth-ford-being-champion-your-own-career

THE LEADER WITHIN YOU

DOI: 10.4324/9781003395034-8

The Leader Within

In 1908, in a small cave near La Chapelle-aux-Saints, France, scientists discovered the skeleton of "the old man of La Chapelle," which was the first relatively complete skeleton of a Neanderthal individual ever found. What I find most remarkable about this discovery is this,

> Scientists estimate he was quite old by the time he died, as bone had re-grown along the gums where he had lost several teeth, perhaps decades before. In fact, he lacked so many teeth that it's possible he needed his food ground down before he was able to eat it. Other Neanderthals in his social group may have supported him in his final years.[1]

The man's companions prepared his food, potentially even pre-chewing it for him, allowing him to eat despite his lack of teeth, showcasing a display of altruism by any measure. What does this have to do with leadership? A fair question, indeed.

Great leaders exhibit specific behaviors and traits. Compassion is one of them. Inborn or acquired, compassion—other-oriented behavior—not only does good, but it raises the level of trust people have in you. And trust is critical to effective leadership.

The Makings of an Effective Leader

Effective leaders listen and take action. They don't just talk.

Bernice Chao is a celebrated trailblazer. She is one of the few female Asian American creative leaders in the industry, working at some of North America's leading advertising agencies. She has created ad campaigns for major national brands, is co-author of *The Visibility Mindset*, speaker, professor, podcast host, and co-founder of the non-profit Asians in Advertising. Chao gives back to the world by fighting against xenophobia toward Asian Americans and inspiring the next generation of talent through mentorship and scholarship programs. Recently, she received an invitation from the White House to be among their esteemed guests celebrating the Chinese New Year. Although still early in her career, Chao already has accomplished what most others take a lifetime to achieve. Clearly, she started thinking and acting as a leader at the outset of her career.

What does it take to think and act as a leader? There are several key behaviors that effective leaders exhibit. Effective, from my extensive experience, means the people who work with you are satisfied enough to work well and collaboratively to fulfill the goals of your organization.

Decency

Call it good character or integrity, no matter what you call it, having decency means you do right by individuals, society, business, creatures, and the planet, desiring positive outcomes for everyone. You consider the impact of your actions.

Disregard for others is dangerous at any time and especially so when someone is in charge. We've seen too many recent examples of leaders without an ethical compass guilty of unprincipled conduct, such as corporate fraud, insider trading, harassment, bullying, embezzlement, corruption, or risky business activities.

A CEO's character is paramount, according to Aiyesha Dey, Høegh Family associate professor of Business Administration at Harvard Business School. Her research suggests,

> ...when hiring CEOs, boards should consider a person's character, with an emphasis on whether a candidate displays signs of materialism or a history of flouting rules. Ignoring those signs and installing a leader whose life away from the office raises red flags can put a company at unnecessary risk.[2]

"Good character is what separates the great from the average, empty words from action, and the successful from the nonsuccessful," writes psychologist Sherrie Campbell.[3]

Dialogue

Listening attentively and responding respectfully are the first actions you can take to get people on board and behind your mission and goals. From my experiences in corporations and higher education, this is a behavior that still needs to be adopted widely. When people climb to leadership roles, whether in mid- or upper-administrative positions, they mistakenly think that telling is guiding, by imposing their vision before any input is requested or given.

There are two basic parts to seeking out what people think and feel. This can happen in group meetings or one-on-one.

1. **Listen to learn.** Genuine listening is not performative nor is it listening to respond, but rather listening to *understand others' viewpoints and learn.*
2. **Listen with regard.** Responding respectfully is critical to the goal of active listening and being respected by others. If your responses are disrespectful, that negates any listening, instead acting to antagonize and harm.

Mindful listening leads to dialogue. Dr. Donald Marks, professor of psychology, in *Strategic Creativity: A Business Field Guide to Advertising, Branding, and Design,* pointed to the crucial distinctions between "dialogue" and "debate." Marks explained that the aim of dialogue is understanding another's perspective. He said, "When one listens to another person in the context of debate, one does so to find holes or flaws in the counterargument. In dialogue, one listens to understand how other people have arrived at their perspectives and beliefs."[4]

This is where the next trait, inborn, existent, or acquired, comes into play, which is being judiciously compassionate when you respond to people's distress.

Wise Compassion

Compassionate leaders care about the welfare of others. They take action to find opportunities and the means to alleviate people's distress. Being compassionate signals a kind of altruism, behaviors that benefit others (with no detriment to oneself). In addition, doing good for others contributes to happiness, according to Laura Santos, professor of psychology at Yale University, who taught the original happiness course at Yale.[5]

Leadership requires the management of an organization and its constituents. A leader is responsible for making tough decisions that are not always popular, clear communication with internal and external constituents, being accountable, solving problems, dealing with crises, and giving critical feedback. These responsibilities demand wisdom, insight, and knowledge of the sector and generally, how things work. When you combine compassion with responsibility, you have a leader who often makes wise decisions. Also, when you combine wise compassion with decency, intelligence, competency, mindful listening, dialogue, well-founded intentions, transparency, and wisdom in the form of insight into people and business (or whichever industry or sector), you have the makings of effective leadership.

> If your actions create a legacy that inspires others to dream more, learn more, do more and become more, then, you are an excellent leader.
>
> —Dolly Parton, singer-songwriter, musician, actor, and humanitarian

Researchers Rasmus Hougaard, Jacqueline Carter, and Nick Hobson discovered a key component of compassionate leadership:

> Compassion on its own is not enough. For effective leadership, compassion must be combined with wisdom...By wisdom, we mean leadership competence, a deep understanding of what motivates people and how to manage them to deliver on agreed priorities. Leadership is hard. To be effective, it often requires pushing agendas, giving tough feedback, making hard decisions that disappoint people, and, in some cases, laying people off. Showing compassion in leadership can't come at the expense of wisdom and effectiveness.[6]

Kindness

Adam Grant, Saul P. Steinberg professor of management and professor of psychology at Wharton, believes that in every organization there are three basic types of people: givers, takers, and matchers (those who attempt to keep an even balance of give and take; quid pro quo). Grant also believes in building a culture of giving, and that the most meaningful way to succeed is to help other people succeed.[7]

You'll remember we examined your values in Chapter 1. Let's revisit values for a moment. In Grant's book, *Give and Take: Why Helping Others Drives Our Success*, he offers these lists of values.

According to Grant, takers favor the values in List 1, whereas givers prioritize the values in List 2.

List 1
- Wealth (money, material possessions)
- Power (dominance, control over others)
- Pleasure (enjoying life)
- Winning (doing better than others)

List 2
- Helpfulness (working for the well-being of others)
- Responsibility (being dependable)
- Social justice (advocating for equality in society)
- Compassion (responding to the needs of others)[8]

"Kind bosses have been shown to increase morale, decrease absenteeism, and retain employees longer. Kind bosses may even prolong the lives of their employees by decreasing their stress levels which improves cardiovascular health," advises psychiatrist Dr. Eva Ritvo.[9]

You can learn about effective as well as poor leadership from the behavior of characters in novels and films. In the film *Tár*, for example, Cate Blanchett portrays the main character, Lydia Tár, who is a world-renowned classical music conductor—a maestro who eventually "faces the music." Kindness is a trait this character does not possess. About Tár's abuse of her power, Justin Davidson writes,

> Conductors charm and wheedle more than they browbeat. Trying to coerce beautiful playing out of resentful musicians is like trying to force someone to love you: inefficient, offensive, and usually counterproductive. Even worse is the conductor who would bludgeon the orchestra into surrendering interpretive creativity and instead demand that players match the version of the score running through her head.

...And the classical-music Establishment, like just about every hierarchical structure, harbors abuse because victims stay quiet and onlookers accept it — until, suddenly, they don't.[10]

The U.S. recognizes the importance of being kind to others by designating February 17th as Random Acts of Kindness Day; I believe kindness should be shown every day in the workplace and beyond.

Transparency and Trust

Being open about the status and future of an organization allows people to see where they fit now and a few years from now. Being honest about any challenges the company is facing is important.[11]

Keeping people in the loop matters, which fosters trust—reliance on someone's character and integrity—and open lines of communication. Building trust starts with any organization's leadership. A leader must establish a safe culture, a healthy environment that encourages open dialogue and transparent communication, which requires authenticity and following through on promises. Remember, a career is a promise.

Leaders should be transparent, trustworthy (don't withhold resources, decisions, or information), regularly provide constructive feedback, encourage respectful dialogue, meet regularly, be authentic and self-aware, reliable, willing to listen and learn from their teams, follow through on promises and commitments, demonstrate inclusion and equity, and be expert enough to share cutting-edge best practices, make informed choices, and move an organization forward.[12]

Equity

Leaders should be counted on to act with integrity and to commit unequivocally to diversity, equity, and inclusion (DEI). Leaders should set and meet an organization's DEI goals by offering equitable opportunities and creating a safe space for everyone to speak up and be heard, as well as taking up advocacy.

Effective leaders take *action to* promote equity, expanding access to those historically excluded, and promoting a sense of belonging for all. One of those actions is hiring diverse candidates. During an interview with Sophie Gold, executive producer of Eleanor, a commercial production company, about the film industry, she advised,

> Don't spend your budget on panels discussing the lack of diversity in the industry. That's performative allyship. Spend your budget hiring BIPOC talent behind the camera as well as in front of the camera. If you want to have BIPOC directors or companies do your work, it's just as simple as giving them your work.[13]

Gold created the only Black, certified female-owned commercial production company in the U.S. She ardently advocates for diversity in the industry so that Eleanor's solo position within it will become one of many.

Equity entails a level playing field, where recruitment, hiring, conditions, opportunities, mentorships, and compensation are fair for everyone.

Cultivating Emotional Intelligence

> The most effective leaders are all alike in one crucial way: they all have a high degree of what has come to be known as emotional intelligence. It's not that IQ and technical skills are irrelevant. They do matter, but...they are the entry-level requirements for executive positions. My research, along with other recent studies, clearly shows that emotional intelligence is the sine qua non of leadership. Without it, a person can have the best training in the world, an incisive, analytical mind, and an endless supply of smart ideas, but he still won't make a great leader.
> —Daniel Goleman, psychologist and author of *Emotional Intelligence*[14]

According to experts, you can develop your emotional intelligence, if you don't already possess it. According to Goleman, the five components of emotional intelligence at work are self-awareness, self-regulation, motivation, empathy, and social skills.[15]

Self-awareness. Some leaders are unaware of how they come across to others. While it might not be possible to be completely objective about your own behavior, it is worth exploring to see if you are working to positively impact people and the workplace. Building self-awareness is a lifelong practice.

Self-regulation. Being able to control your moods, emotions (for example, anger or extreme sadness), or impulses is important because negative impulsive behavior is disruptive in the workplace and potentially destroys progress or amicable working relationships. It's wise to think before you act. One of the best pieces of advice given to me by my father was to be stoic at work, never be unreasonable, or reveal negative emotions that might negatively affect others or yourself.

Motivation. Motivation stems from having passion for your work for reasons beyond money or status, as well as having grit.

Empathy. We've already talked about how important it is to be compassionate, which encompasses being empathetic. Developing the ability to understand other people's situations and feelings in context is the mark of an effective leader.

Social skills. Your ability to navigate interpersonal relationships and social situations allows you to have constructive working relationships with colleagues, supervisors, and stakeholders. That might include dealing with a conflict in a working relationship, having constructive discussions, driving positive results, and conveying your opinions and solutions to co-workers.

Communication

One of the chief pet peeves I hear when I consult is that leaders do not communicate clearly, often enough, or at all.

Speaking in plain language so that everyone understands the nature of any given situation and the necessary actions needed gets more people on board. People emphasize the importance of storytelling, which is critical to engaging communication and building organizations and brands. Story-listening is important, as well. The aim is to listen better. Establishing communication-centered leadership is not only respectful, but it also supports understanding.

Work discussions encompass more than just the topic at hand or the organizational mission; they also involve an individual's sense of recognition, feeling valued by the leader or colleagues for their ideas and contributions.

Put people first, which goes back to leading with compassion. Any organization is a construct; however, each employee is a thinking and sentient individual with ideas, an essence, and rights.

Leading Positive Change

In the past, leaders were primarily focused on pleasing external stakeholders and prioritizing earnings. However, today's leaders must consider the broader impact of their decisions and actions. A worthwhile pursuit involves gains that extend beyond conventional profit, providing value to individuals and society. This concept aligns with the triple bottom line: people, planet, and profit.

Poise Under Pressure

Over the course of your career, undoubtedly you will face challenging situations and obstacles. When dealing with internal or external crises, learning how to maintain your composure will build your leadership skills.

Whether you think of poise as gracious tact or a collected assurance of manner, steadiness in the face of adversity helps everyone, including yourself. This may be a bit of a reach; nevertheless, think of the now-ubiquitous, "Keep Calm and Carry On" Second World War message, which was "one of three key messages created by Britain's wartime propaganda department, the Ministry of Information, for its clear message of 'sober restraint.'"[16]

Personal Leadership Inventory

Aspire to be something bigger, every single day. But it starts by investing in yourself. By learning every day.
—Antonio Neri, president and CEO, Hewlett Packard Enterprise

Which traits of effective leadership do you possess, want to develop, and maintain?

POSSESS
- ☐ Take judicious actions
- ☐ Mindful listener
- ☐ Exhibit decency
- ☐ Engage in respectful dialogue
- ☐ Wisely compassionate
- ☐ Respectful of others
- ☐ Trustworthy
- ☐ Exhibit poise under pressure
- ☐ Clearly communicate
- ☐ Lead positive change

DEVELOP
- ☐ Take judicious actions
- ☐ Mindful listener
- ☐ Exhibit decency
- ☐ Engage in respectful dialogue
- ☐ Wisely compassionate
- ☐ Respectful of others
- ☐ Trustworthy
- ☐ Exhibit poise under pressure
- ☐ Clearly communicate
- ☐ Lead positive change

MAINTAIN
- ☐ Practice transparency
- ☐ Manifest integrity
- ☐ Be accountable
- ☐ Demonstrate resilience
- ☐ Show compassion

Interview: Ilana Kloss

Figure 7.1 Ilana Kloss, CEO of Billie Jean King Enterprises

Photographer: Howard Schatz

Ilana Kloss is the CEO of Billie Jean King Enterprises, where she leads business development and oversees strategic partnerships. From 2001 to 2018, Ilana was the CEO and Commissioner of World TeamTennis, managing both the professional sports league and nationwide grassroots recreational programs. A former world No. 1 doubles player and U.S. Open doubles champion, Ilana is actively involved in the Women's Sports Foundation as a member of the executive board and past WSF board chair. A member of both the National and International Jewish Sports Hall of Fame, she was named Sports Businesswoman of the Year by the Warsaw Sports Marketing Center. Ilana is a part owner of the Los Angeles Dodgers, Los Angeles Sparks, and Angel City Football Club and serves on the executive board of the Elton John AIDS Foundation. She also is a past advisor to the Professional Women's Hockey Players Association.

How did having a mentor support your career?

I met Billie Jean King as a young person, and it changed my life. I was fortunate to be in the room when the Women's Tennis Association (WTA) was formed in June 1973, and it shaped my career. Being a representative in the early days of the WTA was helpful. Billie Jean's leadership style and her mantra for the historic WTA meeting was that she wanted representation from all over the world, every continent, including Africa, where I was from. For me, that spoke to how important different experiences and voices are. Being exposed to this global-looking leadership and learning about the business side of tennis and sports was very helpful and shaped my career path. It's so important to understand all the pieces and not just your specific role. It showed me how important it is to look at everything in front of you and that so often, your career—and the path you take—is bigger than just the role you are playing.

What's the importance of diversity, equity, and inclusion? Of having a level playing field?

It is so valuable to have different voices and people from different backgrounds and experiences at the table. To be effective, you need more than just a seat at the table. You need a voice in the conversation. You never know where a great idea will come from, and I have seen that some of the best ideas often come from outside my inner circle.

A level playing field is a philosophy I always grew up with. My parents encouraged us to be what we wanted to be and not hold back. That's how we lived, and it was so helpful in my career. I learned quickly that the subdominant groups know much more about the dominant group than the dominant group knows about them. We have to navigate that. As a woman, it has always been something we have to embrace to grow and succeed. You must ask for what you want and need.

How did you determine your career path when you transitioned from playing?

I love the sport and the business of tennis. I am fortunate to have relationships I made throughout my career that enabled me to go from on the court to off the court in a field that I knew and that I loved. For me, it was the perfect fit. If you are fortunate enough to be able to work in an industry you love, it becomes a passion and not a job. I was lucky that the birth of women's professional tennis started in my generation, which allowed me to make a living on the court. And, I have been able to continue to make a living off the court, because the relationships you build along your career path are essential to your future growth and happiness.

As a leader in sports, business, and advocacy, any advice on becoming a leader?

Be a mentor and help others. Leadership is a team effort, and no one leads alone. Effective leaders surround themselves with people that care and have similar values. Great leaders open doors, encourage others, and do everything they can to make the team better.

Notes

1　"What Does It Mean to be Human? La Chapelle-aux-Saints," Smithsonian Natural Museum of Natural History, https://humanorigins.si.edu/evidence/human-fossils/fossils/la-chapelle-aux-saints

2　Aiyesha Dey, "When Hiring CEOs, Focus on Character," *HBR Magazine*, July–August 2022. https://hbr.org/2022/07/when-hiring-ceos-focus-on-character

3　Sherrie Campbell, "7 Character Traits Exceptional Leaders Have in Common," *Entrepreneur*.com, October 19, 2017. https://www.entrepreneur.com/leadership/7-character-traits-exceptional-leaders-have-in-common/302773

4　Robin Landa, "Interview with Dr. Donald Marks," *Strategic Creativity: A Business Field Guide to Advertising, Branding, and Design*, 2022: 167.

5　Lindsey Beyer, "Yale's Hugely Popular Happiness Course is Revamped for Teens," *Washington Post*, January 23, 2023. https://www.washingtonpost.com/wellness/2023/01/23/yale-happiness-course-teens/

6　Rasmus Hougaard, Jacqueline Carter, and Nick Hobson, "Compassionate Leadership is Necessary But Not Sufficient," *HBR*.org, December 4, 2020. https://hbr.org/2020/12/compassionate-leadership-is-necessary-but-not-sufficient

7   Adam Grant, "Are You a Giver Or a Taker?" *TED@IBM*. https://
www.ted.com/talks/adam_grant_are_you_a_giver_or_a_taker/
transcript

8   Adam Grant, *Give and Take: Why Helping Others Drives Our Success*, New York: Penguin, 2013: 21.

9   Eva Ritvo, "Can Being Kind Make You a Better Boss? Kindness Works at Work," *Psychology Today*, July 1, 2018. https://www.
psychologytoday.com/us/blog/on-vitality/201807/can-being-kind-make-you-a-better-boss

10 Justin Davidson, "On The Podium: How True to the Conducting Life Is *Tár*?" *New York Magazine*, October 11, 2022. https://www.
vulture.com/2022/10/blanchett-tar-conductor-realistic.html

11 Ami Scherson, "The Importance of Being a Transparent Leader—and How to Be One," CO: U.S. Chamber of Commerce, December 5, 2022. https://www.uschamber.com/co/grow/thrive/how-to-lead-with-transparency

12 Abbey Lewis, "Harvard Business Publishing Corporate Learning Blog: Good Leadership? It All Starts with Trust," *Harvard Business.
org*, October 26, 2022. https://www.harvardbusiness.org/good-leadership-it-all-starts-with-trust/

13 Sophie Gold, conversation between Gold and Robin Landa, August 26, 2022.

14 Daniel Goleman, "What Makes a Leader?" *HBR*.org, January 2004. https://hbr.org/2004/01/what-makes-a-leader

15 Daniel Goleman, "What Makes a Leader?"

16 "History of the University of London: The Story Behind Keep Calm and Carry On," University of London. https://www.london.ac.uk/
about-us/history-university-london/story-behind-keep-calm-and-carry

FINDING FULFILLMENT

DOI: 10.4324/9781003395034-9

What Is Meaningful to You?

"I'm off to save lives," my husband quipped as he headed off to work.

As a physician, he does just that; though his intention with that remark is lighthearted. He works incredibly long hours doing very challenging work, yet he is one of the happiest people I know. Healing people, keeping his patients healthy, and being intellectually challenged fulfill him. Medicine suits his great intellect and curiosity. When I go off to teach at the university or when I write books, I can't say that "I save lives"; however, I do find fulfillment in my career when I see my students succeed.

What Would a Meaningful Career Look Like to You?

Finding work that you believe is worth your investment, addresses your interests, expertise, and aptitudes is worth investigating. Perhaps it's the alignment of all of those elements that leads to finding fulfillment in a career. It's definitely not the same for everyone, nor does it necessarily remain constant over the course of one's life.

> People change. You will change. Don't be afraid of learning new skills because it wasn't what you thought you would be doing.
> —Danny Virasawmi, web designer and developer

In your mind, does "meaningful" denote significant, consequential, substantial, purposeful, challenging (intellectually or physically or both), relevant, groundbreaking, or influential? I can't underscore enough how greatly the definition varies among people. For example, I have friends who are working as creative professionals in design and advertising who love the daily challenge of idea generation and strategic creative thinking; those friends would rather practice their craft, whereas I find meaning in teaching others to practice that same craft.

A talent agent finds meaning as someone who finds appropriate roles for actors and screenwriters, perhaps even greater satisfaction finding roles for those who have been overlooked or historically minoritized. Someone else would find meaning in being "the talent," an actor or screenwriter and not a talent agent.

What You Find Meaningful

To respond to these prompts, make a list of career paths that interest you—whether you list tax accountant or musician, public relations pro or farm animal veterinarian, teacher or editor. Of course, those are just examples—make your own list of three. Then fill in the blanks.

- Your list of possible career paths:

  1.

  2.

  3.

  Respond to the following for all of the career paths you listed:
- I would find being a _____meaningful because_____.
- I would find being a _____fulfilling because_____.
- If I didn't have to worry about income, I would rather be a _____.

Fulfillment Self-Assessment

Satisfaction is important but not totally dependent on your career. Life stressors can adversely affect finding fulfillment at work. Conversely, a satisfying nonwork life makes finding fulfillment at work more possible since you are not unduly stressed otherwise and perhaps actually very happy with a side project, avocation, social group, or hobby. (Dancing is my avocation and provides stress relief and a creative outlet.) The primary goal is to identify how you can achieve and maintain life satisfaction, through your approach, thinking, assessment, and specific actions.

Taking stock will help guide your choices. When you examine work satisfaction and advantages, along with nonwork stressors, then how to find, construct, or augment fulfillment will become clearer.

In the lists below, check off those items that are important to you, whether in a specific job or a career sector. Then scrutinize your list for clues about yourself.

Values:
- (A specific career) aligns with my principles or values
- (A specific career) does not align with my principles or values
- I don't have to compromise my values in this career or organization
- The work reflects my point of view
- The work offers a shared commitment to principles or society
- The work shows evidence of organizational justice
- The work offers regular collaboration
- The work offers collaboration across cultures
- The work offers fair effort-to-reward balance

Challenges:
- Intellectual
- Physical
- Creative
- Frequent problem-solving
- Interpersonal
- Interdepartmental
- Engaging
- Extreme

Talents and Interests:
- My talent is put to use
- I find the work interesting
- (A specific career) is not interesting
- I love this discipline, industry, or sector
- The work is a stepping stone to a career that would utilize my talent or interests

Expertise:
- This is what I studied
- I have the requisite skills
- I want/need to acquire new or additional expertise
- Acquiring the expertise is too difficult (time, money, managing)
- I want to earn certifications
- I'm not well suited to learning this

Significance:
- The work helps individuals, society, business, creatures, or the environment
- The work adds to the conversation (an opportunity to say something different from what others have said before, offering an additional insight or provocation)
- The work is influential or groundbreaking
- The work advances a discipline or sector

Lifestyle:
- Calm
- Fast-paced
- Time for enough sleep; sufficient time away from work
- Time for family and friends
- Travel-related work
- (Have or don't have) decision authority at work
- (Have or don't have) social support at work

Personality:
- The work aligns with my personality traits, e.g., extroversion, agreeableness, open to experiences, conscientiousness
- The work doesn't work well with my personality or personality derailers, if any, e.g., excitable, perfectionistic, impulsive

Overall Life Satisfaction in Work Domain:
- Work
- Health
- Compensation
- Growth
- Family
- Social relationships
- Self-worth

- Leisure time
- Work–life balance
- Time for interest in other life domains, e.g., art, music, working out, the outdoors, or political or social activism

Overall Life Satisfaction in Nonwork Domain:

- Health
- Financial situation
- Family
- Social relationships
- Self-worth
- Leisure time
- Work–life balance
- Time for interest in other life domains, e.g., art, music, working out, the outdoors, or political or social activism

Chronic Stressors:

- Persistent compromised health
- Multiple family or social roles
- Caregiver role
- Discrimination
- Lack of options
- Daily life issues
- Housing conditions
- Lack of housing
- Lack of resources
- Relationship with partner, parent, or child
- Life events, e.g., divorce, layoff, death or illness of a relative, partner, or friend
- Transportation issues
- Other types of life distress

Endeavors That Would Add Breadth or Satisfaction to Your Life:

- Creative
- Intellectual
- Community service
- Political
- Physical
- Brand new pursuit
- Long-held aspirations or ambitions (something you've always wanted to attempt).

Finding Fulfillment Outside of Work

Put bluntly, many organizations are interested in what you can contribute and produce, and not in your passion or purpose. Some companies might take advantage of your dedication and passion for their own ends. Although it's ideal to find purpose or passion in your work, it's not always possible. At times, work is simply work in the most fundamental form. That's why I highly recommend finding some fulfillment outside of work. It's easier to do than you might think.

Finding fulfillment outside of work makes you more tolerant of work—more energized if it's something you enjoy. Having an alternative interest in a different or related domain or path that provides joy allows for a greater sense of self. "First, shift one activity away from work to something that will provide meaning to you outside that realm. Second, be more intentional in small moments with others to make lasting social connections. And third, lean into transitions and commit to forcing change in those times even when it feels uncomfortable," advises Rob Cross, Edward A. Madden professor of Global Leadership at Babson College and the co-founder and director of the Connected Commons.[1]

Passion Projects and Side Hustles

A *passion project* is a piece of work or project outside of your chosen career that you explore out of interest or passion, often not in order to earn income. It's a side project that brings benefits; it might make you feel happier and more productive in your career work. For example, if someone is an attorney, they might embark on making a film using their smartphone or camcorder.

A *side hustle* is similar, but your main motivations are earning an extra income and exploring new opportunities. A passion project can lead to a side hustle and even a new business. As a side hustle, my friend sought discarded furniture on the street and refurbished the found items to sell or use. He turned that side hustle into a "green" furniture retail business to supplement his joy and income. Finally, he gave up his full-time job to open a vintage, green furniture retail store.

A passion project or side hustle can put your interests and skills to another use. They are opportunities to explore possibilities.

According to a recent Zapier survey, one in three people—34 percent—in the U.S. have a side hustle, and 24 percent plan to start one. But money isn't the only motivator. Nonfinancial reasons for starting a side hustle include:

• Do something fun, or something people enjoy
• Develop new skills
• Test a specific business idea[2]

According to Amanda Pressner Kreuser, co-founder and managing partner at Masthead Media Company, "It's not uncommon to think that launching a side business will be at odds with your full-time job—but that doesn't need to be the case. Often the skills you have gained throughout your career will help you build your business. But even more so, this side hustle can improve how you show up in your 9-to-5 role, too."[3]

When I asked PJ Pereira how one of his passions, martial arts training, has benefited him beyond fitness, he replied that having multiple life domains and an identity as a martial arts "fighter," which is an identity beyond his advertising career, is critical to his well-being. Not entrusting one's whole sense of self and identity to a career is wise. He said,

> The world taught us that the thing directly after your name is your profession, which means that your identity gets associated with your craft. Therefore, any bump in your professional life is a strike to your self-esteem, is a strike to your sense of self-worth. Protecting that is very important.
> (Read the full interview with Pereira in Chapter 1)

Identifying a Passion Project or Side Hustle

Check off which of the below items apply to you, and see where your checkmarks lead.

☐ I need to express my creativity
☐ I need to express my emotions

- ☐ I want to challenge my intellect
- ☐ I want to employ my talent that goes untapped at work
- ☐ My secret hobby is:_____
- ☐ My avocation is:_____
- ☐ I want a fresh and exciting challenge
- ☐ I want to break rules and go beyond conventional thinking
- ☐ I secretly aspire to be:_____
- ☐ I want to test a business idea or product
- ☐ I want a canvas/opportunity/setting that shows the real me
- ☐ I crave independent work and autonomy
- ☐ I would welcome an opportunity to make a difference in my community
- ☐ I would welcome an opportunity to supplement my income through an engaging pursuit
- ☐ I want to make or build a _____ _____
- ☐ I want to invent/create/write a _____ _____
- ☐ I want to volunteer on behalf of a social cause or charitable organization
- ☐ I want to do my civic duty
- ☐ I want to be among like-minded people

Eoin McLaughlin on Careers

Figure 8.1 Eoin McLaughlin, deputy executive creative director of 4creative and children's book author

Eoin is deputy executive creative director of 4creative, the in-house agency at Channel 4 in the U.K. A public service broadcaster, it is regularly cited as one of the most influential brands in the world. Its work to support the Paralympics has won two D&AD Black Pencils and three Cannes Grand Prix. The Prime Minister called it "genius."

He is also a bestselling children's book author. His books have been translated into 25 languages and twice named "Books of the Year" in *The Guardian*. Previously Eoin worked at Droga5 in New York. Before that, he was a garbageman.

Care.

Don't sign away half your life just so you can update your LinkedIn profile.

If you do something you actually care about, you'll be better at it. You'll have more fun. And you'll end up more successful (by any sane measure of the word).

Or just take the highest paying job you can find, go home every night and stare into the abyss.

Follow People Around.

(Not in a creepy, stalker-y way. *Please* don't do that.)

But if you go and work with thoughtful people who do cool stuff, then you are more likely to *be* a thoughtful person who does cool stuff. Sounds simple. And it kind of is, but in all probability, at some point, it will involve making some tough life decisions.

Like watching your friends earn more money. Like turning down a promotion. Like moving to Dundee.

But it will pay off in the end. Dundee is actually very pretty.

Give It Away.

If you are miserly with your good ideas, you will have less of them.

If you help other people, and don't really care about who gets the credit, more good stuff will happen.

I don't really understand it, but it's true.

Be Kind.

"Kindness" is a word rarely found in job descriptions. This is one of the great insanities of the modern workplace, because along with a brain, and a very basic level of competency, empathy is your most important attribute. Sensitivity is not a weakness; it's a superpower. It's not about being meek or avoiding difficult situations; in fact, empathy actually puts you in the best position to deal with all that stuff. You might occasionally feel you lose out in individual circumstances, through a lack of wolfish ruthlessness, but overall, you'll win. Other kind and talented people will want to work with you again and again over the course of your career.

Be Thoughtful.

Think before you do stuff.

Ask for other people's opinions before you decide on your own.

Get interested. Read. Go to the factory. Talk to people that know more than you.

And please, for the love of God, don't do what everyone else is doing.

Make Stuff Happen.

Lots of people have good ideas.

Not many people make them happen.

In the words of the Greek goddess of victory, just do it.

And NEVER EVER give advice. It makes you sound like a pretentious know-it-all.

Oops.

Small Joys and Deep Fun

Did you know that a Yale University course about happiness is one of the most popular in the university's 320-year history? In her "Psychology and the Good Life" course, Dr. Laurie Santos, the Chandrika and Ranjan Tandon professor of Psychology and head of Silliman College at Yale University, teaches students the common misconceptions about happiness, what really does improve our well-being, and strategies to become happier.

According to Santos, "You'll also learn that self-care—doing things to boost our own well-being—often comes from focusing on others and doing something nice for the people you care about," adding that implementing "strategies to savor the small things—that morning cup of coffee or a nice shower" are invaluable small steps toward improving your well-being.[4]

"By using evidence-based practices like these," said Santos, "we've shown empirically that people tend to show a significant boost in happiness after taking the class."[5] Many people don't realize that changing small behaviors, rather than their circumstances, can increase joy. Rather than expecting happiness to come from life's big moments, you can focus on a daily practice of small joys. Of course, happiness is somewhat subjective.

Positive psychology expert Stella Grizont noted, "But nearly every [happiness] expert we surveyed emphasized the same cocktail of ingredients: a sense of control and autonomy over one's life, being guided by meaning and purpose, and connecting with others. And they largely agreed that happiness can be measured, strengthened, and taught. 'The more you notice how happy or how grateful you are, the more it grows.'"[6] Happiness experts recommend behaviors and activities such as having a personal hobby (art, writing, music, cooking, gardening, gaming) and spending time with friends outside of an office or professional setting, among others.[7]

One way that I have found joy at work is to focus on small wins and accomplishments. Take a moment to acknowledge a job you've done well or a team effort that went well.

Fun at Work vs. Deep Fun

Many employers earnestly offer what they consider engagement opportunities at work. I would venture to say most employees seek opportunities for engagement at work, too. There are many ways to have fun at work. "Research suggests that fun has a positive impact on employee engagement, creativity, and retention," according to Bob Nelson, PhD, a leading worldwide advocate for employee recognition and engagement.[8] As examples, Nelson advocates that it can be restorative to make a game of the tasks on your to-do list; switch things up for a fresh perspective by making simple changes, such as calling your "to-do list" a "fun list"; and vary your location to a temporary one, such as a coffee shop.[9]

For deeper engagement, employers should investigate and understand how "people experience their organization day by day."[10] If you're seeking deep fun or deeper engagement, get involved in bigger engagement challenges, such as redesigning the interior workspace, rethinking work practices, or offering efficiency tips on how to better manage the day-to-day workflow.

Daniel Coyle—author of *The Culture Code*, and advisor to many high-performing organizations, including the U.S. Navy SEALs, Microsoft, and Google—advocates "deep fun," where engagement is deeper, more challenging, and employees take more ownership of their work experiences.[11]

Thinking Creatively

Count the number of women artists' works represented in any art museum's European Gothic, Renaissance, Mannerist, Baroque, Rococo, Neoclassical, Romantic, or Naturalism/Realism period galleries. You will be doomed to disappointment.

If you believe that an individual's innate talent will transcend a society's conventions and obstacles, again, you will be doomed to disappointment.

During those eras, women interested in painting or drawing were not allowed to be apprentices in other artists' studios. They were not permitted access to life drawing classes or to fine art materials. However, there were a few women who painted and sketched, for example, Artemisia Gentileschi, who was an Italian Baroque painter. How did she manage that? Born in Rome, Artemisia was the only daughter of painter Orazio Gentileschi, under whom she trained. Rarely would a woman have access to apprenticeships, as did Italian Renaissance portrait painter Sofonisba Anguissola. Born in Cremona, Italy, because her father was progressive, Anguissola was trained as a painter by Bernardino Campi, "Perhaps because her gender precluded her from studying anatomy or working with nude models, she focused on portraiture, often turning to sitters in her familial and social circles."[12]

Now extend systemic sexism to race, ethnicity, and religious beliefs, and take another walk through those European galleries. So, no; creativity (or genius) doesn't outweigh opportunity or hegemony.

For other myths about creativity and innovation, blame hokey films and melodramatic operas and novels. Romanticized notions have misinformed us. Even children are not spared being witness to animated stories that depict children or adults creating in a fit of inspiration. Creativity myths mislead us into thinking that only a select few possess a golden nugget of artistic genius, which spills out in "Eureka!" moments.

Sure, some people's personality factors lend to creative thinking. Research psychologists Guillaume Fürst, Paolo Ghisletta, and Todd Lubart determined an integrative model of creativity and personality. The personality factors they cited are: *Plasticity* (high openness, extraversion, energy, and inspiration), *divergence* (low agreeableness and conscientiousness, high non-conformity and impulsivity), and *convergence* (high ambition, precision, persistence, and critical sense).[13] However, anyone can learn to be open, curious, and persistent in dealing with the ambiguities inherent in the creative process.

> The constant happiness is curiosity.
> —Alice Munro, Nobel Prize-winning writer

Uncertainty and Ambiguity

As PJ Pereira explained in his interview in Chapter 1, many people shy away from creative thinking due to the inherent uncertainty of the creative process.

Becoming comfortable with ambiguity is one way to unlock your creative potential. Being open to more than one interpretation when solving a problem using creative thinking also enhances your chances of generating a creative solution or idea. In a study of parents and their adolescent children, "Tolerance of ambiguity was significantly and positively related to creativity."[14]

If you recognize that the creative process involves uncertainty and ambiguity, then you also recognize that it lends itself to not defaulting to a reliance on past experiences, preconceived, or used ideas or solutions. Peter Himmelman, Grammy- and Emmy-nominated singer-songwriter, visual artist, author, film composer, and entrepreneur, explains why ambiguity is good for your creativity,

> While I may struggle with ambiguity, that struggle demands that I stay alert and am constantly improvising. By allowing myself to work inside ambiguity, I prevent myself from falling back on musical ideas that are already known to me. It's true, I will, for a time at least, be floundering—lost at sea as it were. But it's in "getting lost" that I will call upon greater reserves of mental awareness in order to make a successful song out of my map-less musical meanderings.[15]

Thinking Creatively Tips

To awaken your creativity, adopt the following traits of great creative thinkers:

- Be open to new experiences and possibilities.
- Listen and observe attentively to notice potential.
- Be curious about many different subjects. If Lin Manuel Miranda hadn't been curious about early U.S. history, we wouldn't have the musical *Hamilton*.
- Ask "What if?" questions.
- Learn to live with ambiguity.
- Learn how to generate ideas.
- Travel and/or immerse yourself in different cultures.

Interview: Lee-Sean Huang

Figure 8.2 Lee-Sean Huang, co-founder and creative director of Foossa; director of Design Content and Learning at AIGA; and host and producer of AIGA podcasts

Lee-Sean Huang is a Taiwanese American designer, artist, and educator. He was born in Kaohsiung, Taiwan and grew up in the Phoenix, Arizona metropolitan area. He now splits his time between Providence, Rhode Island, and New York City. In 2013, he co-founded the service design and strategy practice, Foossa. Since then, he has collaborated with communities and organizations across the Americas, Europe, Africa, and Asia to address social innovation challenges. He has taught design, innovation, and storytelling at New York University, the Parsons School of Design, and the School of Visual Arts. He currently serves as the senior director of Design Content and Learning at AIGA, the oldest and largest professional association for design in the United States. His artistic practice includes photography, performance, and audiovisual media. His current creative focus on street photography and environmental portraiture grew out of the ethnographic research and documentation work that he carries out in his design practice. Lee-Sean earned a Bachelor of Arts degree in Government from Harvard College and a Master of Professional Studies in Interactive Telecommunications from New York University's Tisch School of the Arts.

How did you determine your career path and purpose?

My career path has been more intuitive than intentional. I never set out with some sort of master plan or purpose statement for my career at the beginning.

For me, a lot of the dot-connecting and meaning-making happens in retrospect. I basically followed the fun and the learning. I didn't quite have the words for "follow the fun" until I saw an interview with multi-hyphenate actor, rapper, writer, producer Donald Glover, where he explains his diverse career and creative outputs as the result of following the fun. Like Glover, I've made choices and chose projects that I thought would be fun. In addition, I have also been attracted to jobs, gigs, and projects where I think I will learn something from the experience. Beyond "am I having fun," and "am I learning," I also periodically check in with myself and ask these simple, but not easy questions:

Am I making a difference here? Are we doing good? Am I leaving things better than I found them?

Your work is at the intersection of design and democracy. Would you please tell us about your career in designing participation and building movements?

My work at the intersection of design and democracy is sort of the synthesis of my bachelor's degree in political science and my master's degree in interactive media design, and my professional experiences in-between and since. For me, design and democracy are both about power and how we manage trade-offs. A design project may be initially about aesthetics and usability of a product or service, but ultimately, it's about power, whether it's at the micro-level of empowering the individual users of the product or service to accomplish their goals or at the macro-level of designing business models that shift economic or cultural power from incumbents to entrepreneurial insurgents.

I also have an expansive definition of democracy. While free and fair elections and respect for fundamental rights are of course the cornerstones of a democratic society, democracy is also about an open and creative culture. With this broad definition, there are plenty of opportunities for designers to get involved.

Early in my career, I worked in advocacy communications for environmental and humanitarian issues. This is how I got into doing design professionally, as I found myself figuring out HTML and Photoshop to create email blasts and communications materials for our campaigns. I then decided to go to grad school to get more formal, structured training in design. And while I was in grad school, I ended up interning at a creative agency and strategy consultancy called Purpose. I was their first in-house design hire, and ended up building out their design team after they hired me full-time after I graduated. At Purpose, we were building online campaigns and movements around all sorts of issues ranging from beauty standards for women and girls to promoting sustainable transportation to advocating for international LGBTQ rights.

I learned that design plays a role in all of that, not just in creating individual assets or pieces of creative that are used in a campaign, but we also design narratives and strategies, and ways for people to get involved creatively, whether it's inspiring people to organize their own house parties or rallies around an issue or getting them to contribute to the public conversation with their own user-generated content.

After a few years at Purpose, which also gave me the opportunity to work in places like Brazil, India, and all over Western Europe, I decided it was time to strike out on my own.

I started Foossa with my partner David Colby Reed. At Foossa, we call our work "community-centered design," which is really a mindset and an ethos of collaboration and participation, designing with and not just for the people who will be using what we make. Since starting Foossa, I've had the opportunity to work in a lot of different spaces, from helping UN agencies better manage their institutional knowledge and tell their success stories to working with local government and community organizations to provide more effective financial counseling to New York City residents. I have also been teaching design for more than a decade now, so I also see my role as shaping the next generation of citizen-designers.

You've collaborated with communities and organizations across the Americas, Europe, Africa, and Asia to address social innovation challenges. What advice can you offer about fruitful collaboration?

I feel like my thoughts on how to collaborate with diverse global communities on social innovation challenges could fill an entire semester's course or certainly a book, but either way, it comes with a big "it depends" disclaimer. Every community, every organization, and every situation is different. However, it's always a good idea to start with humility. We need to get past the "designer knows best" kind of arrogance that has led our profession astray so often. Our collaborators already have a wealth of expertise in their own context. We are there to build on and with that, not to teach them some generalized "best practices" that can come across as arrogant or even colonial. In addition to designing for the core challenge that we were invited to tackle, I also see the job as designing touchpoints and opportunities for mutual exchange and learning.

Beyond humility, and I know this is going to sound cliché but stay with me, we need to immerse ourselves into the context and really look and listen to our collaborators and stakeholders. Digging even deeper, it's not just about observing and taking notes, it's about building a model to help us understand WHY people say what they say and do what they do. What are their motivations? What makes them tick? Designers have a lot to learn from social science and the dramatic arts when it comes to exploring motivations and mental models.

Friction is not always a bad thing. It can be a reminder to slow down and make sure you are aligned with your collaborators. Or it can be the opportunity to pause and learn more. Similarly, conflict can also serve the same purpose as friction in terms of helping us learn and grow along with our collaborators.

As a leader in design, any advice on becoming an early leader?

My advice for aspiring leaders is to first understand the different aspects of leadership, and then you can figure out where and how you can bring value. From my perspective as a leader in design, I see at least three non-mutually exclusive aspects or archetypes for being a leader: the manager, the mentor, and the muse.

The manager may be the first and most obvious aspect of leadership. Whether you are the creative director, CEO, or commander-in-chief, it's about being responsible for people, practices, and outcomes. This is the kind of leadership that comes from paying your dues and demonstrating your ability to take on progressively more responsibility. It's about being very organized, seeking advice and expertise when needed, and weighing the trade-offs when making hard decisions.

A manager may also be a mentor, but not always. Mentors can give advice, share perspectives, and sometimes open doors to opportunities, but they don't necessarily have to directly manage or be responsible for your work in that way. While mentorship often happens one-on-one in private conversations, there are other times where you may not even know you were a "mentor." This could be something you said online or in a published interview that reached someone who needed it, and it helped them grow and progress creatively or career-wise.

This brings us to the muse, who like a mentor can be providing their leadership directly in a one-on-one relationship, or more indirectly from afar. A muse provides visionary ideas, stories, and creative concepts. This might be one of the few times your creative work can speak for itself. Maybe it's something you wrote, or a story you told, an artwork you made, that resonates beyond your immediate circle and inspires someone else to shift their perspective somehow, to think about things in a new way, to make their own creative work. Maybe that's a kind of thought-leadership too.

My point is that leadership is more expansive than just "management," so the sooner you realize this, the more freedom you will have in finding your unique way of being a leader.

What's the best career advice anyone has ever given you?

The best career advice I got was deceptively simple and decidedly not profound hidden knowledge. It was basically, "keep going," but it was exactly what I needed at the time. In the early days of starting Foossa, the social innovation design practice that I co-founded, I had the opportunity to do a mentoring session with Alexis Ohanian, a tech entrepreneur and investor who got his start as one of the founders of Reddit. Alexis asked me questions about our practice, and basically said that it seemed that I was on the right track and that I should just keep on doing what I was already doing. For me at the time, that was just the bit of validation that I needed to continue. Going your own way and forging your own path can be lonely and scary, so that kind of advice really mattered to me. Advice doesn't always need to be about strategy, it can just be encouragement. It reminds me of one of my favorite French expressions, "bonne continuation," which literally wishes someone "good continuation," or more idiomatically in English, "keep it up." Or I picture Tim Gunn from *Project Runway* saying, "alright, carry on!" So, if you are reading this right now and you need the encouragement, let me say to you, "keep on going, keep it up, keep on making."

Notes

1   Rob Cross, "Do You Have a Life Outside of Work?" *HBR*.org, May 13, 2020. https://hbr.org/2020/05/do-you-have-a-life-outside-of-work

2   Zapier editorial team, "One in Three Americans Have a Side Hustle," *Zapier*.com, January 14, 2021. https://zapier.com/blog/side-hustle-report/

3   Amanda Pressner Kreuser, "How to Balance Your Passion Project with a Full-time Job," *Inc*.com, July 16, 2022. https://www.inc.com/amanda-pressner-kreuser/how-to-balance-your-passion-project-with-a-full-time-job.html

4   Jenna Romaine, "The Pursuit of Happiness: Yale's Free Courses on How to be Happier Sees Unprecedented Surge During Pandemic," *The Hill*, January 11, 2022. https://thehill.com/changing-america/well-being/mental-health/589211-the-pursuit-of-happiness-yales-free-course-on-how/

5   Jenna Romaine, "The Pursuit of Happiness: Yale's Free Courses on How to be Happier Sees Unprecedented Surge During Pandemic."

6   Angela Haupt, "The Happiness Revival Guide: The Daily Habits of Happiness Experts," *Time*.com, January 5, 2023. https://time.com/6241099/daily-habits-happiness-experts/?utm_medium=email&utm_source=sfmc&utm_campaign=newsletter+brief+default+ac&utm_content=+++20230108+++body&et_rid=206308851&lctg=206308851

7   Angela Haupt, "The Daily Habits of Happiness Experts."

8   Bob Nelson, "Ascent: Why Work Should Be Fun," *HBR*.org, May 2, 2022. https://hbr.org/2022/05/why-work-should-be-fun

9   Bob Nelson, "Ascent: Why Work Should Be Fun."

10 Jacob Morgan, "Why the Millions We Spend on Employee Engagement Buy Us So Little," *HBR*.org, March 10, 2017. https://hbr.org/2017/03/why-the-millions-we-spend-on-employee-engagement-buy-us-so-little?utm_campaign=hbr&utm_source=twitter&utm_medium=social

11 Daniel Coyle, "The Importance of Deep Fun," DanielCoyle.com, January 3, 2018. http://danielcoyle.com/2018/01/03/importance-deep-fun/

12 John Marciari, transcription, "Sofonisba Anguissola," The Morgan Library. https://www.themorgan.org/exhibitions/online/van-eyck-to-mondrian/sofonisba-anguissola

13 Guillaume Fürst, Paolo Ghisletta, Todd Lubart, "Toward an Integrative Model of Creativity and Personality: Theoretical Suggestions

and Preliminary Empirical Testing," *The Journal of Creative Behavior*, June 2016; *50*(2), 81–164. https://doi.org/10.1002/jocb.71

14 Franck Zenasni, Maud Besançon, and Todd Lubart, "Creativity and Tolerance of Ambiguity: An Empirical Study," *Journal of Creative Behavior*," Creative Education Foundation, 2008, 42, 61–72. https://www.researchgate.net/publication/253935530_Creativity_and_Tolerance_of_Ambiguity_An_Empirical_Study

15 Peter Himmelman, "Why Leaving the Familiar and Embracing Ambiguity is Good for Your Creativity, *Forbes*.com, May 20, 2019. https://www.forbes.com/sites/peterhimmelman/2019/05/20/why-leaving-the-familiar-and-embracing-ambiguity-is-good-for-your-creativity/?sh=4529d1447502

MAKE A PLAN

Resources:

Your time in hours per week:

Action plan: What needs to be done and in what order and by when:

Index

Pages in *italics* refer to figures.

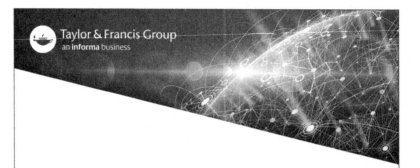

Printed in the United States
by Baker & Taylor Publisher Services